Escape from Happiness

ESCAPE
from
HAPPINESS

George F. Walker

Coach House Press
Toronto

This play is fully protected under the copyright laws of
Canada and all other countries of the Copyright Union
and is subject to royalty. Changes to the script are
expressly forbidden without written consent of the
author. Rights to produce, film, record in whole or in
part, in any medium or in any language, by any group,
amateur or professional, are retained by the author.
Interested persons are requested to apply for
permission and terms to:

Great North Artists Management, Inc.
350 Dupont Street
Toronto, Ontario, Canada M5R 1V9

The punctuation of this play carefully
adheres to the author's instructions.

Published with the assistance of the Canada Council,
the Ontario Arts Council, and the Ontario Ministry
of Culture and Communications.

Canadian Cataloguing in Publication Data
Walker, George F., 1947-
Escape from happiness

ISBN 0-88910-440-9

I. Title.
PS8595.A55E7 1992   C812'.54   C92-093317-3
PR9199.3.W35E7 1992

Contents

Introduction

In 1982, while I was running a small theatre in New York City, a friend gave me a collection of plays by a Canadian writer. It contained a one-act play called *Beyond Mozambique*. In the first scene an enraged German doctor, exiled to the darkest jungle, rips a human foot from around the neck of his native assistant, screaming, 'Have you no respect for human dignity.' He then hurls the foot into the bushes. At that moment, I thought to myself, 'I must get to know this writer.'

Since then, my relationship with George F. Walker has included directing six productions of four different plays, a collaboration in adapting one of his plays to a screenplay, and, most recently, directing the first American production of *Escape from Happiness* at New York Stage and Film at Vassar College. I should say up front that I consider Walker to be one of the most remarkable playwrights now working in the English language, and *Escape from Happiness* an amazing, in fact a *great*, play.

Walker has never shied away from the complexity and paradoxical nature of human experience; in *Escape from Happiness*, he has written a play whose strong narrative through-line keeps the audience delightedly engaged while its breadth leaves room for the substantial development of ten highly individual and original characters.

Essentially, it is the story of how a family—the same family that appears in Walker's *East End Trilogy*—comes together to meet

7

an outside threat. The anger, familiarity, love, and tension with which the family members interact among themselves and with strangers, provide the heart and humour of the play.

Having worked with Walker on *Better Living*, one of the East End plays, when I first read *Escape from Happiness* I looked to Nora, the mother, to sound the major thematic chords of the play. Happily, within the first ten pages or so, she also gave me the key to the plot: 'This is the story of my son-in-law's vicious beating.' Throughout our work on the script and rehearsals, keeping that simple sentence in mind was of exceptional importance: Junior's beating, the event that opens the play—understanding why it happened, who was behind it, and what must be done about it—was the prime directive in moving forward with the story-telling. Whenever a tricky point came up in rehearsal I would say to myself, 'Keep telling the story of Junior's beating,' and eventually we would find our way back to what felt right for the production.

At our first rehearsal I asked the question, 'Why do this play?' For many of us who work in the theatre, the answer to this question often has to do with finances or with career advancement—it is rarely addressed as part of the work process. Even for those theatre artists who think in terms of their own personal expression, however, it is important to develop a group sense of mission in relation to a new play.

I had chosen two speeches with which to start the discussion, and I quoted them for the cast. First, Dian:

> It's big this thing we're engaged in! Big and contradictory. It's new and old. Woman and man. Daughter and father. Smart and dumb. Really, really smart! And really, really dumb!! See you tomorrow, partner.

I felt that Walker, among other things, was writing a message to all of us in the production. Throw out your conceptions of what is right or good for a play. Work on my stuff like you work on life, like it's this big thing we're engaged in that we don't know a lot about until we're in it.

Second, Nora's speech:

> We're running away from happiness. We think we need to struggle, and suffer, and work really hard before we can just stay still, and let happiness catch up and surround us.

At first I interpreted Nora's words as a critique of Western culture—of the great Judeo-Christian myth of transcendence through suffering that still rules our society and our individual lives. That if there is a free, joyous, happy place for human beings to live in, we can only come to it by experiencing the real pain and rage that being human entails. But Nora rarely criticizes anything directly, let alone her family's outlook; ultimately, her words are descriptive. They also contain a contradiction: Why would we have to work and struggle and suffer in order to let something catch up and surround us? If we're pushing a boulder uphill, we usually don't consider that the real work may come in letting it go. The 'escape from happiness' is not necessarily a bad thing to Nora—it may be too bad, but it's just what it is—precisely the kind of contradiction that Walker has always insisted on as the stuff of life.

The philosophical fault lines that separate men and nations increasingly include the acceptance or rejection of contradiction, vividly demonstrated in America recently by Robert Bork's nomination for the U.S. Supreme Court. In stating his judicial philosophy, Bork argued that any increase in the rights of a minority results in the diminution of the rights of the majority. Freedom of choice diminishes the society's right to regulate reproduction; affirmative action diminishes the majority's right to jobs; gun control diminishes the right to bear arms. Such logic leads to conclusions such as, More food for you means less for me, Japanese wealth implies Western poverty—a linear and simplistic view of the world that takes as its prime hypothesis that 'A' and 'not A' cannot co-exist.

We need only examine our own inner landscapes of thought and feeling to reject this hypothesis: in the reality of our lives, opposites and contradictions crowd one another in glorious confusion. It is in accommodating and accepting these opposites that the real, hard work of individuals and social systems takes place. Indeed, when we try, as individuals, to remove the inherent contradictions and complexities of life, we risk vacuous sentimentality or intractable pigheadedness. A society taking the same course invites fascism. Indeed, while accepting Justice Bork as an intelligent, able and well-qualified legal scholar, the Senate Judiciary Committee, when confronted by his philosophy, rejected his nomination on the grounds of his ignorance and lack of compassion as a man.

In *Escape from Happiness*, Walker attempts to cut the historical connection between passion and coercion. I have had many conversations with him about the complicated relationship of his country and mine, and I think we both dream—with Nora—of a society that would combine Canadian acceptance and inclusion with American passionate aggression. A contradiction, you may say—except perhaps for an artist who understands that human beings are capable of talking about human dignity while throwing a freshly severed foot into the bushes. To me, a love/hate relationship with mankind is the common bond that links artists throughout history. *Escape from Happiness* opens that wound, cleanses it with laughter, and puts it on display to console and terrify and challenge its audience all at once. For that we owe a great debt to the playwright.

Max Mayer, New York, 1991

Escape from Happiness

Production History

Escape from Happiness was first produced by New York Stage and Film Company in association with the Powerhouse Theatre at Vassar College, Poughkeepsie, New York, in July 1991.

Producing Directors: Leslie Urdang, Max Mayer
    and Mark Linn-Baker
Associate Producer: Tom Kelly
Director: Max Mayer
Set Designer: Tom Lynch
Lighting Designer: Donald Holder
Costume Designer: Paul Tazewell
Production Stage Manager: Ruth Kreshka
Cast: Jane Kaczmarek, Alexandra Gersten, Ilana Levine,
    Suzanne Shepard, Mark Hammer, Deborah Hedwall,
    Victor Arnold, Dan Moran, James Villemaire,
    Joseph Maselli

Escape from Happiness was first produced in Canada by the Factory Theatre, Toronto, in February 1992.

Producer: Dian English
Artistic Director: Jackie Maxwell
Director: George F. Walker
Production Designer: Peter Blais
Lighting Designer: Michel Charbonneau
Musical Score: Leslie Barber and Shirley Eckhard
Fight Coordinator: John Stead
Stage Manager: Paul Mark
Cast: Nancy Beatty, J.W. Carroll, Oliver Dennis, Barbara Gordon,
    Susan Hogan, Frances Hyland, Ken James, Eric Peterson,
    Jane Spidell, Greg Spottiswood

Persons

NORA
ELIZABETH, *Nora's oldest daughter*
MARY ANN, *Nora's middle daughter*
GAIL, *Nora's youngest daughter*
JUNIOR, *Gail's husband*
TOM, *the father of Nora's daughters*
DIAN BLACK, *a police detective*
MIKE DIXON, *a police detective*
ROLLY MOORE, *a criminal*
STEVIE MOORE, *a criminal*

Place

The worn-down kitchen of an old house in the east end of a large city. A screen door leading to the backyard. A door leading to the basement. A doorway to the rest of the house. An old fridge and stove, a table, four or five chairs, a broom closet, and a pantry. And all the rest of the usual kitchen stuff.

Note

There are two intermissions, the first between Scenes Three and Four, the second between Scenes Five and Six.

Scene One

Lights up very fast
JUNIOR *has been beaten up. His clothing is torn. He is bloody. He is on his back on the floor.* **GAIL** *has his head in her lap.* **NORA** *and* **GAIL** *are wearing coats. There are bags full of groceries on the counter and the floor. A couple of chairs have been turned over.* **NORA** *is holding a baby wrapped in a blanket in one of her arms. And she is on the telephone*

GAIL Tell them to hurry, dammit!

NORA [*into the phone*] Hurry, dammit! [*she hangs up*]

GAIL Junior, what happened. Who did this to you. God Mom, look at him. It looks serious.

NORA He's not hurt badly. If he was hurt badly there'd be a certain kind of smell in the air. Sure he looks weak and torn up, but that's just the way he looks. Can he talk. Ask him if he can talk.

GAIL Can you talk.

[**JUNIOR** *groans*]

NORA Did he say something.

GAIL He made a sound.

NORA That could be a good thing. That could be his way of letting us know he's alive.

GAIL What are you talking about. He's alive. He's breathing, isn't he.

NORA I meant alive in a deeper way. Sure he's breathing. But inside has he given up. Is there hope and lightness in his heart. I'm nervous. I'm not sure I'm saying exactly what I mean.

GAIL I can't believe this. We were only gone an hour. A little shopping. My first time out of the house in weeks. We come home and find this. Shit ... Junior, who did this to you?! [*to* **NORA**] Call 911 again.

NORA No, you can't do that. It annoys them. Also, they get confused and suspicious. I've heard terrible stories about their confusion. We'll just have to hope and pray a reliable person took my call. Ask him to make another sound. Ask him if he feels alive.

GAIL Junior. Can you hear me. Can you say something.

JUNIOR [*groans*] What? [*mumbles*]

[GAIL *has her ear to* JUNIOR*'s mouth*]

NORA What's he saying.

GAIL He's saved.

NORA That's what he said? He said, 'I'm saved'?

[GAIL *puts her ear to* JUNIOR*'s mouth again*]

GAIL No. Not saved. Afraid. He said he's afraid.

NORA That's different than saying, 'I'm saved.' Emotionally. There's a whole world of difference between those two statements, Gail. Try to be more specific. How can I help if you don't translate properly.

GAIL Is that what you're doing. Helping?! How? How are you helping.

NORA I'm ready to help. It depends on him. On his state of mind. If he wants or needs a change in his state of mind to sustain life, I'm ready. Ask him if he thinks he's dying.

GAIL No.

NORA Ask him. Make it clear. Don't mumble. Separate every word. Make sure he understands. Do it. It's important.

GAIL I can't.

NORA It's important.

GAIL You do it. I can't!

NORA He might lie to me. I'm his mother-in-law. We have an interesting relationship, but I'm not sure it's built entirely on the truth. Ask him if he thinks he's dying. Do it before it's too late, Gail.

GAIL Junior. Are you dying ... Are you dying?!

JUNIOR [*weakly*] Yes.

[NORA *grabs* GAIL *and pulls her away. She kneels beside* JUNIOR]

NORA Junior! Junior! Can you hear me. This is Nora. This is your wife's mother. This is your child's grandmother. I want you to do something for your wife and your child. Junior! You have something to do. If you don't do it the people you love will be destroyed. Destroyed! Did you hear me. You'll be destroying your young, innocent family. Junior! Here's what you have to do. You have to get up.

GAIL Mom!

NORA Don't distract me, dear. Get off that floor, Junior! Get off that floor!

GAIL Mom, please. He's bleeding to death. He's probably got internal injuries. He's—

NORA Get up, Junior! You're killing us here! You're killing us with your misery. We need you to get up. Your baby wants you on your feet. Hear her crying for her daddy? [*she pinches the baby. The baby cries*]

GAIL What did you just do.

NORA [*whispers*] I pinched her. [*she pinches the baby again*]

GAIL Stop that! Stop doing that. What's wrong with you.

NORA Junior, do you hear your baby crying! She's crying because she wants you to get up. She's saying, 'Daddy, Daddy please get up. Daddy, please, please don't die on that floor!'

GAIL Stop it.

NORA Junior! Daddy! Junior!

[JUNIOR *groans loudly. He tries to sit up*]

GAIL No. Don't make him do this. Junior, lie down.

JUNIOR I gotta get up! [*he sits up*]

NORA That's not good enough. Look at yourself. You're on the floor. We need you off the floor.

JUNIOR Off the floor. Oh my God. Jesus. I gotta— [*he is struggling to his feet*]

NORA Thatta boy.

JUNIOR Gotta get off the floor. Why? Why off the floor.

NORA Because you're alive. You're not dead. The floor is for dying. You have to avoid that floor. Defeat that floor. Rise above that floor! Get up!

JUNIOR Okay. [*he staggers to his feet. weakly*] Okay. I'm up. What now.

GAIL The ambulance is on the way.

JUNIOR I'm dizzy.

GAIL Here. Lean on me.

NORA Stay away from him. He's on his own. If he leans, he falls eventually.

GAIL Can I get him a chair.

NORA No chair. Talk to him if you want. Ask him questions he can answer. Simple ones.

GAIL Junior. What time is it.

JUNIOR What? What's wrong with you. Look at me. I'm dying!

NORA Junior! Dance!

JUNIOR What?

NORA Dance. Do a slow dance ... Gail, turn on the radio. Turn it on now!

[GAIL *turns on the radio. She begins to search for appropriate music*]

Find some nice music. Be patient, Junior. Music is coming. There. That's good. Now dance, Junior!

[JUNIOR *is moving slowly. An ambulance siren sounds in the distance*]

Ambulance is coming, Junior. Help is on the way. The police, too. Fire department. Everyone is coming to help. We're not alone, Junior. Life goes on ... [*to* GAIL] He's going to be all right.

[*The ambulance is getting closer. Closer.* GAIL *takes the baby from* NORA. NORA *starts to unpack the groceries.* JUNIOR *is still dancing. Lights flash outside*]

[*Blackout*]

Scene Two

NORA *is sitting across the table from* DIAN BLACK. DIAN *is a police detective, neatly, pleasantly dressed. She is about thirty-five.* MIKE DIXON, *her partner, is standing a few feet away, hands in his pockets. He is older, tougher looking. At this moment, he doesn't appear interested in what* DIAN *and* NORA *are saying. He is casually looking around the kitchen*

NORA This is irregular procedure. I'm not an expert in these matters. But I have some knowledge of police procedure, and this is irregular. I'm a citizen who reported a crime. Maybe you're just being innovative, but it appears I am being questioned as if I were suspected of something. If you're not being innovative, maybe you're just confused.

DIAN You said you have some knowledge of police procedure. [*long pause*] Well?

NORA I'm sorry. Was that actually a question, dear.

DIAN Yes.

NORA Well dear, were you actually asking me how I got such knowledge.

DIAN Yes. How did you get such knowledge.

NORA My husband was a policeman.
[DIAN *looks at* MIKE. MIKE *nods*]
[*to* MIKE] You knew my husband?

MIKE Yeah. Worked the fraud squad with him.

NORA That's nice. I think his two years on the fraud squad were the happiest years of his life. I don't know why exactly. Wasn't for any reason a normal person could understand. He's dead now, of course. Has been for several years. I'm sorry if this comes as a shock to you.

MIKE I saw him on the street last week.

NORA That's a man who looks remarkably like him. He lives here in my house. He behaves like my husband, and to some degree like the father of my children. But my husband

19

is dead. Don't get me wrong. This man isn't really an imposter. He's just dangerously confused. Does any of this help you with your investigation.

MIKE No.

DIAN [*looks at* MIKE. *to* NORA] It's too early to say.

NORA It wasn't too early for him to say. He said no.

DIAN [*smiles*] Well, he's wrong.

   [DIAN *and* MIKE *look at each other.* MIKE *shrugs. He begins to look around the kitchen again*]

NORA Well, here we are again. In a state of irregularity. All I've done is call the police to report a crime. My son-in-law is lying in a hospital bed because he was viciously beaten.

DIAN By two men.

NORA Two men. White. One young. One … older.

MIKE [*has obviously been only half-listening*] Black guys?

NORA No.

MIKE Oriental guys.

NORA No.

   [DIAN *looks at* MIKE. *She frowns*]

MIKE Asian guys. Guys in turbans? [*he gives* DIAN *a 'what's your problem?' look*]

NORA No. White men. I don't know what they had on their heads. I suppose they could have been wearing turbans. But that would have been odd. Odd enough that he certainly would have mentioned it.

MIKE He said they were white? He actually described them as white.

NORA No. I know them.

DIAN You know them?

NORA Sort of.

DIAN Sort of?

NORA I know them sort of only as white.

MIKE What does that mean. You know them only as white. Sort of. Is there a possibility they could be something else.

NORA I don't think so. I'm not an expert on criminal

behaviour. I have some experience. But I'm not a criminologist or anything like that. Are there criminals running around out there, white criminals who sometimes appear black. Or black criminals who sometimes appear white.

DIAN We think that drugs are involved. Your son-in-law has a history of drugs, doesn't he.

NORA You must be talking about someone else's son-in-law. My son-in-law was a car thief. He has no involvement with drugs. He has a child. And up to the very moment he had his child he was a child himself. I believe I should call a lawyer. I know several of them. My oldest daughter is a lawyer. I could call her. You'd like her. Well, perhaps you wouldn't like her, but you'd respect her. She'd insist on that. Because she worked very hard, overcame so many obstacles to become what she is.

DIAN You don't need a lawyer, Nora. You're not being charged with any crime.

NORA Well, that clears that up. Not that I was worried. But you've been so vague. Intentionally vague. Almost arrogant. I know you probably don't think so. I've had police people in my house for dinner. In their hearts they're normal people, most of them. But they have an arrogant manner. You serve them a good meal. They just look at you in a funny way. You try to understand what that look means. Does it mean the food's cold. That there's not enough of it. That they expect you to put it directly into their mouths. I don't know. Maybe you could take this opportunity to explain that look to me right now. I mean, it all ties together with our conversation here. And your attitude towards my son-in-law. And perhaps even your attitude towards visible minorities and the way they dress.

MIKE [*approaches slowly*] You were hospitalized once, weren't you. I remember Tom mentioning something. That was a few years back … So how'd that go. How are you doing these days. Do you ever go back to that hospital.

NORA [*to* DIAN] My husband had me committed once, dear. [*to* MIKE] She didn't know what you were talking about. I could tell from her expression.

MIKE So ... how are you.

NORA I'm fine. I've learned a lot since that happened. First, I learned that I wasn't insane. The doctors in that hospital told me that right away. They talked to Tom. They thought he was insane. They were right. I'm a grandmother now. I got to be a grandmother by bringing my children up to the point where they could have children. It wasn't easy after your good friend Tom deserted us. But that's another story. This is the story of my son-in-law's vicious beating.

DIAN On the surface, Nora. At first glance. To the uniformed police officers who came here to your house earlier, that's what it probably appeared to be about.

MIKE But we're different. Our job is to go farther.

NORA Farther than what. I mean, how far ... can you go.

MIKE As far as we want.

DIAN He means ... we have information those policemen in uniform don't have. We specialize in taking that information and applying it in various ways to apparently random events in order to find possible connections, patterns ... systems, an ... organization of events ... Organizations ... That's the area of our expertise.

NORA You're experts? I'm fond of experts, usually. I admire their devotion. What are you called. What's your official name. The outline you gave is impressive. At first. That's the first impression. That it's ... impressive. But once you think about it— Well, you could be anything. You need a name.

MIKE O.C.S.

DIAN Organized Crime Squad ... And in this house, Nora— the house where you live with your youngest daughter and her child, where a man who looks like your husband also lives—your son-in-law is possibly—make that probably—

performing and arranging to be performed, a variety of criminal activities.

MIKE These are drug-related activities. These are prostitution-related activities, pornography-related activities, money-laundering-related activities ...

NORA Distantly?

MIKE What was that?

NORA Distantly related? Or ... closely related. Distantly related could be just a product of rumour. Neighbourhood gossip. There are dozens of religious fanatics on this street. They report people all the time. They reported me once for abusing my daughters. My daughters had some kind of virus that made their eyes swell up. The fanatics told the police I'd been poking them in the eyes with heated knitting needles. I had to get a letter from a doctor. Show it to the police. Circulate it in the neighbourhood. When they're wrong about people, the fanatics just smile and say, 'Better safe than sorry.' Of course they're in for a very large surprise. Because they're all going to rot in hell.

[*Pause.* MIKE *and* DIAN *look at each other*]

DIAN Yes. Well, we don't rely on rumours. We use investigation. Surveillance ... [*she looks at* MIKE] Good judgement. You see, Nora, Junior's a ... a ... a ...

MIKE He's a crook. He keeps company with other crooks. The beating he received was a payback. A deal went wrong. Money was owed. Junior was to blame. At this moment I'm assuming you know nothing about this. Call it a hunch.

DIAN [*to* MIKE] A hunch? ... Oh yeah, I forgot. You get ... hunches.

MIKE Something wrong?

DIAN [*smiles*] No ... No, I agree. I think Nora doesn't really know much about Junior. Even if she believes deep in her heart that she does. It's natural that a grandmother would give the father of her grandchild the benefit of any doubt.

[GAIL *comes in from the hallway. She sees* MIKE *and* DIAN]

GAIL Ah, shit.

NORA Something wrong, dear.

GAIL Yeah. They're still here. Can't you get rid of them. Can't you tell them to just get the hell out. Don't they have something else they could be doing. You know, maybe something useful for a change ... Shit.

[*She leaves*]

MIKE Who was that.

NORA My youngest daughter. Gail.

MIKE So, what's her problem.

DIAN She hates cops, obviously. Right, Nora.

NORA Yes.

DIAN Any particular reason.

NORA Lots of particular reasons. For one thing, she believes being a policeman is what turned her father into a monster.

MIKE Well, that's just stupid. Get her back in here. I'll straighten her out.

DIAN That won't be necessary.

MIKE Says who. Besides, we should question her. Just because I've got a hunch about the mother here doesn't mean I've got the same hunch about her kid.

DIAN I'm afraid he's right, Nora. We don't have to question her now, but Gail's involvement will have to be determined at some point. We can assume only so much.

MIKE Listen, we don't have to tell you any of this. What we assume. Or don't assume. About who. Or what. We're doing it because you're Tom's wife. And Tom was a good cop.

NORA Tom's dead! And he was a good cop but a lousy father. A neglectful, bitter parent. I'm a good parent, relative to him, anyway. You'll have to remember that if you bring trouble to my family. If you remember that, you'll understand my anger and why I'll be trying to destroy you ... I'm sorry I said that. That wasn't me talking. Not really.

24

That must have been some dark part of my soul talking. Forget what I said. You just do your police work and everything will be fine. That's what we have to believe. That the positive will win out. That the dark parts of a mother's soul won't be awakened. I have to go now. Is that permitted during this kind of procedure. In this irregular, but obviously condoned way of doing things, am I permitted to leave you.

DIAN Yes.

MIKE Sure.

NORA Thank you. [*she stands*] I'll just go upstairs. I have something productive to do up there. I'm wallpapering the bathroom.

[*She leaves. Pause*]

DIAN So?

MIKE So? What?

DIAN What do you make of her.

MIKE She's a fuckin' flake. They'll be putting a net around her any day. When she talks, my skin crawls. I get a headache. I don't want anything to do with her. If we have to interrogate her again, you do it alone.

DIAN What's your problem. Does she remind you of someone in your past or something.

MIKE Did I say that. You're out of line.

DIAN Just curious. Is it common for you to have such an emotional personal response to people.

MIKE You're way out of line. They've told me about you. I think we should keep our relationship professional.

DIAN I'm a professional. Don't worry. Didn't I handle that interrogation in a professional manner.

MIKE Not really. No. I thought you were kind of weird with her. Kind of friendly or something. Like you were trying some ... new approach. Maybe it's the approach I've been told to watch out for. It's something new. No one knows exactly what it is. But it's new. And no one likes it.

DIAN I have degrees in sociology and urban planning. Could that be what you're talking about.

MIKE I don't know. Maybe. Why'd you tell me that. What's that prove. It's like you're always trying to prove something to me. Impress me or something.

DIAN I think police work is just an expression of my need to participate. A way to use my education to interact fully in the human experience.

MIKE I don't want you interacting with me. Let's get that straight. First of all, I'm married.

DIAN You think I'm interested in you sexually. You're old enough to be my father. Actually, you remind me a lot of my father. Maybe that's why I have these strange, ambivalent feelings about you. Relax. I'm just thinking out loud now.

MIKE Hey, hey! Come on, I was just saying I get enough interaction. People questioning my motives. I've got a family that does that all the time. You're just my partner. We're cops looking for crooks. That's it.

DIAN That's part of it. The rest of it is we're human beings. We need a certain degree of self-awareness, or we can't do our jobs properly. For example, if you remind me of my father, you should know that. It might help you understand the way I relate to you. Here's another example. When I ask you for an opinion about a suspect, and you launch into an obsessive whine about how that suspect gives you a headache and makes your skin crawl, I feel it's important to find out why. I think maybe she reminds you of your mother. If that's the case, it's something you need to deal with.

MIKE You can't talk to me like that. You wanna know why? Because I don't understand what you're saying. Also, it freaks me out. We've got a job to do here. We can't be freaking each other out. You've got to cool it with that stuff. I'm freaked already. I'm so freaked I can't stand to be in the same room with you. I'm gonna wait in the car. [*he starts off*]

DIAN Hold on a minute. Talking about professionalism, what was all that about black guys, Asian guys, guys in turbans.

MIKE Questions. They were just questions.

DIAN Incredibly insensitive questions. Surely you're aware we have an image problem in that area. Our attitude to racial matters is publicly suspect. You do read the newspapers occasionally, I assume. Because if you don't, if all you do is follow your ... hunches, well you're just not aware enough to do your job properly.

MIKE Look, just shut up. Don't talk to me anymore. If you keep talking to me we're going to have a serious problem. All I know is I've got a hunch, yeah that's right, a *hunch* that something's going on in this house. And I'm gonna get a search warrant. A good, old-fashioned search warrant. [*He leaves*]

DIAN [*throws her arms in the air. She starts off, talking to herself*] Yeah, get a search warrant. Get a couple of attack dogs, too. Hey, why not get the whole fucking army! [*She is gone.* NORA *sticks her head in. Looks around. Comes in. She is carrying a roll of wallpaper. She goes to the screen door. Then over to the table. Sits. She looks worried. She begins to mumble to herself. Slowly we realize she is replaying her scene with the two cops. We catch the odd key word, recognize a gesture, a movement. After a moment* GAIL *comes back in, holding* TOM *by the arm.* TOM *moves slowly. His head is bowed. He has a blanket around him.* GAIL *helps* TOM *towards a chair*]

GAIL Thanks for getting them out of here. The smell of them was filling the house. [GAIL *helps* TOM *sit. She gets a box of crackers from a cupboard. Sits next to him. Gives them to him one at a time. He eats slowly*]

NORA They left on their own. In their own good time, I think.

27

They were so irregular. So full of tension. The world out there is getting worse by the minute. And the police are being affected. Their nerves are frayed. Their minds are disintegrating.

GAIL Why'd you let them in the house. They had no right being here in the first place.

NORA I was just being polite. They began by being polite. I was just returning their politeness.

GAIL Well, now you know.

NORA Now I know what, dear.

GAIL You let people in this house all the time. Total strangers. Derelicts. Crazy people. You have to stop. This is a good time to stop.

NORA What are you saying, Gail. Are you saying they weren't actually the police, that they were just crazy people pretending to be the police.

GAIL No. What I'm saying is smarten up. It's time to just stop trusting everyone. Cops included. They're out to get us.

NORA Everyone? Is everyone out to get us.

GAIL No! Yes! Yes. Just assume everyone's out to get us. Keep the door closed to strangers. And if those cops show up again, keep them out. Call someone.

NORA I'll call Elizabeth. She'll know what to do.

TOM Who's Elizabeth.

GAIL Elizabeth is your oldest daughter, Dad. She's a lawyer.

NORA Gail. Please. I've asked you a hundred times not to call this man Dad. [*she goes to the fridge. Starts to clean it out and rearrange things*]

GAIL I'm not having this argument with you anymore, Mom. If you don't want to admit he's your husband that's your business. But he's my father. He's Mary Ann's father. And he's Elizabeth's father.

TOM Mary Ann?

GAIL Your other daughter. You see Dad, it goes like this ... Try to pay attention, I'm getting sick of telling you.

Elizabeth is the oldest, then Mary Ann. Then me. I'm Gail.
I'm the youngest.

TOM Why don't the other two ever come around.

GAIL They come around when you're asleep, Dad. They don't
like you.

TOM Was I mean to them.

GAIL Yes, you were.

TOM Was I mean to you.

GAIL Yes. You were mean to me, too.

TOM But you're here all the time.

GAIL I forgave you.

NORA Oh sure, you forgave him. You even transformed him.
You took a total stranger and made him into your flesh and
blood. It was an act of incredible imagination and perhaps
even generosity. But Gail, I have to ask you, where is it all
leading. What good can come from it.

TOM [points to NORA] She'll never forgive me.

GAIL You got that right.

TOM Does she know I'm dying. Maybe if we tell her I'm dying
she'll forgive me.

NORA Tell him I know he's dying. And I'm sorry. He's a
human being. I feel genuine sadness over the dilemma of
death as faced by all human beings. But also tell him that's
beside the point.

TOM There's misery in this house. I can feel it. Is it because of
me. It usually is.

GAIL Junior was hurt, Dad.

TOM I know Junior. He brings me soup.

GAIL Junior was beat up by a couple of guys. We don't know
why.

TOM Bastards. Were they bastards.

GAIL Yeah. And now the cops are on our back. They think
Junior is involved with these guys in some criminal gang or
something.

TOM Bastards. Bastard cops. Bastards.

NORA Don't let him get started.

TOM Bastardization! I've had experience with all those bastards. The crooks, and the cops, and their bastardization of the simple, real world that was constructed by simple, real people. I like Junior. He brings me soup, and unsalted crackers. [*he stands*] If you see him, send him my best. I've got to go back to bed now. I'm upset. [*he starts towards the door to the hall. Stops*] Junior's not here?

GAIL No, Dad. He's in the hospital.

TOM If I need soup, who'll bring it to me.

GAIL I will.

TOM Good. And crackers … And some juice. The fizzy kind. With a straw, if it's no trouble.

[*He leaves*]

NORA Go watch him. Make sure he doesn't go into my bedroom.

GAIL He knows where his room is.

NORA Go watch.

[GAIL *goes out to the hall*]

He forgets. He says he forgets. Sometimes he's in my bed. Under the covers. Naked. I have to sleep down here in the living room. I'm getting scared. Do you think he wants a sexual experience.

GAIL Well, not tonight. He's in his own room.

[MARY ANN *and* ELIZABETH *appear at the screen door*]

MARY ANN Is he gone.

GAIL Yes.

ELIZABETH Go check.

GAIL I just did. He's gone to his room. For the night.

ELIZABETH Go make sure.

MARY ANN Go make sure he's not listening at his door. That he's actually going to bed.

GAIL No.

ELIZABETH Go check, Gail.

MARY ANN We're not coming in until someone goes up there

and tells us he's in his bed.

NORA Please, Gail. We need them to come inside. We need to talk together as a family. We can't talk about the things we need to talk about through the screen door.

ELIZABETH Look, we're not staying out here indefinitely. We're leaving.

MARY ANN She's right. We're leaving. Or we're coming in. But we're only coming in if someone actually goes up there and checks him out.

NORA [to GAIL] Please, dear.

GAIL Unbelievable.

[She goes out]

NORA This should only take a second. How are you both.

ELIZABETH Fine.

MARY ANN I'm okay, Mom.

NORA How's your daughter, Mary Ann.

MARY ANN She's great, Mom. She misses you. She said to give you a kiss. She said, 'Give gwamma a beeeg kiss-kiss.' She said, 'I miss gwamma. I want gwamma.'

ELIZABETH Shut up!!

MARY ANN That's what she said.

ELIZABETH She said 'gwamma'?

MARY ANN Yeah.

ELIZABETH Well, she's four years old. Teach her how to say it properly.

[GAIL comes back]

GAIL He's in bed. He wants split pea.

ELIZABETH He wants what?

GAIL Soup. He likes soup. That's basically all he likes.

NORA You can come in now.

[They come in. ELIZABETH heads for the telephone. Takes a pad from her briefcase. Punches in her code. Writes down her messages]

Will you make his soup for him, Gail.

GAIL That's what I'm doing, Mom. That's why I opened the

cupboard. That's why I took out this can.

NORA [*to* ELIZABETH] Junior usually makes his soup. But Junior— But, well, Junior … You better tell them, Gail.

GAIL I told them already, Mom. I called them and told them. That's why they're here.

MARY ANN Where's your daughter.

GAIL Upstairs. Asleep. Where's yours.

MARY ANN At home. What do you mean. She's at home, of course. She's asleep, too. What do you mean, Gail. What were you getting at.

GAIL Nothing. Relax. You asked about mine. I asked about yours.

NORA That's what sisters do. They ask each other things. It's great. I always feel great when you're all together asking each other things. Telling each other things. I can't tell you how it makes me feel.

GAIL Sure you can. It makes you feel great.

ELIZABETH How come Dad only eats soup. Is he getting worse.

GAIL Yeah.

MARY ANN Has he seen a doctor lately.

NORA Now, why would Gail want to talk about that. Talk about a man who, to be kind about it, may or may not be her actual father, when her actual husband is lying in the hospital fighting for his life.

MARY ANN His life?

[ELIZABETH *hangs up the phone*]

GAIL No. He's all right. He's going to be all right. Broken arm. Ribs. Cuts and stuff. Mom, why do you do that. Make outrageous exaggerations like that.

NORA To get attention, perhaps. To bring the truth into focus. To provide a starting point for conversation. Something to be agreed with or disagreed with. To get things rolling. Something like that. Tea anyone? Sit down. Everyone sit down. Except you, Gail. You just continue making the man upstairs his soup. And make sure you serve it at just the right temperature. I know you will, though. I know you deeply respect his needs. [*to* MARY ANN] She deeply, deeply respects his needs ... for some reason.

MARY ANN She feels sorry for him, Mom.

ELIZABETH Yeah, Mom. She's like you that way. She has sympathy for the diseased and dying.

GAIL He's my father.

ELIZABETH So what. He's my father, too. And do you see me taking care of him. I'd like to throw him off the fucking roof.

MARY ANN You see, Mom, we all feel our own way about him. Elizabeth hates him. I'm afraid of him, and Gail feels sorry for him. And that's okay. It has nothing to do with you. It's not directed at you. Any of it.

NORA He's in my house. He eats my food. Uses my furniture. And my bathroom. Occasionally sleeps in my bed.

GAIL By accident.

NORA So *she* says. But, well, I'll give her that one. That one is too distressing to discuss in detail. We'd have to explore the darkest part of human sexuality.

ELIZABETH We can have him moved out, Mom.

MARY ANN We can find a home for him.

NORA You'd go to all that trouble. And expense. You're wonderful people. So compassionate. To extend yourself so badly for a *total* stranger.

ELIZABETH Mom, please.

NORA I know. I know. That man upstairs says he is your father. And you all have a tremendous inner need to believe him.

ELIZABETH And you have a need to not believe him. We respect that, Mom.

MARY ANN We agreed to that, Mom. We agreed to let you not believe. And you agreed to let us believe.

NORA But from an historical perspective, Mary Ann—it's

hard. You see, historically, your actual father deserted us and left us in a wretched hole of poverty and debt. And then ten years later a man just ... showed up. The man upstairs. *Why?* Whoever he is, why is he here. It's a simple question. But the answer could be historically terrifying. It scares me. I can't sleep. I'm thinking of taking pills. Lots of pills.

GAIL Oh, stop it. You're fine. You don't see him much. You never talk to him. You can deal with it. He stays. I want my kid to know her grandfather. I want her to have roots.

NORA Okay. Forget it. I'm *fine* ... if she says so—

ELIZABETH [*to* GAIL] Whatya mean roots. She doesn't need roots from that jerk. He's her grandfather, but he's slime.

MARY ANN Anyway, she's got us. We're her roots.

GAIL You're never here.

MARY ANN We're here.

GAIL You sneak in at night for a few minutes. Give Mom a hug, then piss off. When's the last time you saw Gwen.

MARY ANN Who's Gwen.

GAIL Gwen's my daughter's name, you asshole.

MARY ANN Please be nice to me. I've made so much progress in the last few months. I'm a much stronger, more independent person. But I believe my strength and independence are entirely dependent on people being nice to me. So does Clare.

GAIL Who's Clare.

ELIZABETH Her therapist.

MARY ANN My friend ... My therapist and my friend. Mom. I have something to tell you.

GAIL Not now. [*to* ELIZABETH] Please don't let her get started.

MARY ANN I have knowledge. It's important knowledge, and I want to share it with my mother. With you too, Gail.

GAIL No. Look. I guess you guys have forgotten why I called you. We're in a bit of trouble here. You know. Junior. The crooks. The cops.

ELIZABETH Don't worry. I'm looking into it. I've called my contacts on the police force.

NORA I thought everyone on the police force hated you, dear.

ELIZABETH Most of them do, I guess. Ignorant, Neanderthal bastards can't take a little constructive criticism.

NORA [*to* GAIL] Elizabeth has recently been publicly critical of the attitudes and practices of the police in several sensitive areas.

MARY ANN We know, Mom.

GAIL She's a first-class shit-disturber.

MARY ANN We're all real proud of her.

GAIL Right. But now we've got to—

ELIZABETH Don't worry. When I've got time I'll call my contacts back. See what they found out.

MARY ANN Mom. Gail.

GAIL When you've got time?

MARY ANN Gail. Mom. Listen. I have to share this knowledge with you. I've always shared my knowledge with you. All of you.

ELIZABETH And that's what's made us the people we are today.

MARY ANN Elizabeth is a lesbian.

ELIZABETH What.

MARY ANN You're a lesbian. And you're proud of it. And I'm proud of you for being proud. And now Mom and Gail can be proud of you, too.

ELIZABETH Mary Ann, what are you doing.

MARY ANN I'm outing you.

NORA What, dear?

MARY ANN I'm outing her. She's been in the closet. I'm helping her get out. She's a lesbian. Say it loud and clear. She's a lesbian. She's a lesbian! Clare told me to do it. Someone did it to Clare, and it was the best day of her life. So I'm doing it to you, Elizabeth. You're a lesbian. You have sex with women. Lots of women. Lots and lots of women. Right?!

35

ELIZABETH [*to* NORA *and* GAIL] Let's talk about Junior.

NORA We went to see him in the hospital.

GAIL There were two cops guarding his door. I mean, come on—they think he's some kind of criminal mastermind.

NORA I'm worried, Elizabeth. The beating was unprovoked. Junior was alone here. They broke in and beat him for a reason Junior doesn't know.

ELIZABETH Or isn't telling.

GAIL He doesn't fucking know. Okay? We got that straight? We can move on from that?

ELIZABETH Yeah. Okay. He doesn't know.

MARY ANN [*pointing at* ELIZABETH] Lesbian!

ELIZABETH Look, what's your problem.

MARY ANN It won't work unless you admit it. Admit it, and let us all hug you and love you. Lots and lots and lots.

ELIZABETH If I admit it, do you promise not to hug and love me lots and lots and lots.

MARY ANN Whatever.

ELIZABETH Okay.

MARY ANN Say it.

ELIZABETH I'm a lesbian.

MARY ANN Tell Mother.

ELIZABETH Hey, Mom. I'm a lesbian.

NORA I know, dear.

ELIZABETH She knows.

MARY ANN She knows? For how long.

ELIZABETH Forever, you silly cow. You're the only one in this family who didn't know.

MARY ANN Why. Why am I the only one who didn't know. Why. Tell me.

ELIZABETH Guess.

MARY ANN No. Tell me. Why didn't you tell me. How come Clare had to tell me.

ELIZABETH *Your* therapist told you I was a lesbian?

MARY ANN Yes. Clare told me. She says you're famous in

lesbian circles. You're a famous lesbian. She told me to be proud of you. So I am. Not that I wasn't before. But now I am, too. But more so.

ELIZABETH Why? Why more so?

MARY ANN Because it was hard.

ELIZABETH What was hard.

MARY ANN Being a lesbian.

ELIZABETH Get another therapist. One who will concentrate on *your* problems.

MARY ANN Wasn't it hard.

ELIZABETH Your life's falling apart. You've been a basket case for almost twenty years, and you sit around talking to your therapist about me ... Amazing ... Now tell them. Stop talking about me, and tell Mother and Gail what's new with *you*.

MARY ANN Not yet.

ELIZABETH Tell them. Or I will. And I won't make it all sad and gooey like you will.

MARY ANN I'm leaving my husband.

GAIL Again?

MARY ANN I have to. I'm at a crossroads. How many times does a person come to a crossroads.

GAIL If they're like you, about every three months.

NORA What about your daughter. Is she with Barry.

MARY ANN Larry. Yeah. He loves her. He'll be good to her. He understands my needs. He understands me.

GAIL Great. Maybe he could explain you to us.

ELIZABETH He doesn't really understand her. I asked him once. Actually, I begged him. I begged him to explain to me what makes her tick. He just shook his head and whistled. And then he made the sound of a loon.

MARY ANN You should talk to Clare. She could explain me to you. She explained me to me ... Okay. This is the thing. I'm a kindred spirit of all the victims of the women's holocaust. A once powerful gender-species decimated by the religious patriarchy because they were terrified of their feminine strength.

GAIL What the hell is she talking about. And why is she talking about it now!

ELIZABETH [*smiles. To* MARY ANN] A witch. Are you saying you're a witch.

MARY ANN I would have been a witch if the witches hadn't been decimated. [*to* NORA] The way it is now, I don't belong anywhere. I'm at a crossroads, though. I'm ready to belong somewhere. And the thing is, I've always admired Elizabeth so much. Elizabeth has always been my strength. So I'm thinking maybe I'll become a lesbian, too.

ELIZABETH You see, that's why I never told you. I knew you'd pull some kind of wacky shit like this. This is not something you choose.

MARY ANN I think you might be wrong. Clare showed me some statistics.

ELIZABETH All right. It's something *you* shouldn't choose. I made a choice. But all your choices are wrong. So you shouldn't choose!

MARY ANN That's not fair!

GAIL [*suddenly bangs the pot of soup down on the stove, hard*] Okay! That's it. That's enough! I mean, come on. Junior's in the frigging hospital. And there are cops swarming all over our lives here.

NORA Mary Ann. I don't like saying this, but you leave me no choice. You could go to hell and rot there for eternity if you don't stop deserting that child of yours.

MARY ANN I'm not deserting her. I'm at a crossroads!

GAIL [*bangs the pot*] Hey! Shut up! Shut the fuck up! I didn't call you here to listen to this garbage!

MARY ANN It's my life!

GAIL Your life is a joke!! [*she starts to bang the pot over and over again*]

ELIZABETH Okay!! Okay!! That's enough!! I haven't got much

time. I've got three court appearances tomorrow, a letter to the editor I have to write, and a poor, sick bastard I'm trying to get committed! I'm very, very busy! Let's deal with this Junior thing, whatever it is.

GAIL You're always very, very busy. I'm just asking a little advice from you. If you can't spare the time to help your family, get the hell out!

ELIZABETH Listen, kid. Watch your attitude. I'm here, aren't I?!

MARY ANN And so am I!

NORA But that could be a mistake, Mary Ann. You're here. But is there somewhere else you should be instead. Perhaps somewhere in the vicinity of the innocent, little child you brought into this world.

MARY ANN Please, Mom. Don't keep doing this. You have no right to say those things to me.

[GAIL *throws her arms up. She goes to the table. Sits. Puts her head down*]

ELIZABETH She's your mother. She's just expressing an opinion.

MARY ANN But it's so morally loaded. Isn't it. It's so dense with … guilt. And stuff. Guilt and remorse. She can say whatever she wants, but she can't—

[TOM *appears at the doorway*]

TOM Hey, where's my soup.

MARY ANN Oh my God.

[*She runs into the basement*]

TOM Where's she going. Who is she.

ELIZABETH Get him out of here.

TOM Who are you.

ELIZABETH Get him out of here. Or I'm history.

GAIL [*looking up*] Go back to bed, Dad. The soup is coming.

TOM Is this woman one of mine. She looks like me, I think. Shouldn't we be introduced.

GAIL This is Elizabeth, Dad. Your oldest daughter. You know

her. You've just forgotten.

TOM Sure. I remember now. I've forgotten. [*to* ELIZABETH] Hi. How you doin'. Come here. Give me a hug.

ELIZABETH Okay. That's it. I'll be out back. Let me know when this clown's back in his bed. You've got five minutes. [*She goes out back*]

NORA Tell him to leave, Gail. Tell him he's causing turmoil.

TOM Well, that's obvious! I forget things but I'm not, you know ...

GAIL I'll be right up, Dad.

TOM The thing about soup is the temperature. You know, just like the porridge in *Goldilock*. Think of me as Baby Bear. That's what I always tell Junior. Any word about Junior.

GAIL He's going to be fine. Thanks for asking.

TOM Well, as long as he dresses warmly and puts his wages in the bank. If he does that, Alaska can be a friendly, profitable place. Besides, the world needs that pipeline. You should be proud of Junior for helping to build it. When his plane gets in send him upstairs and we'll have a little chat. [*He leaves*]

NORA Everything he says has a purpose. Don't ever let him convince you otherwise. That man has a reason for being here, and a reason for everything that comes out of his mouth.

GAIL [*has a small tray prepared. She goes to the counter. Pours the soup into a bowl on the tray*] He's sick. He's got a disease that's done something to his mind. That's all there is to it. I'll take him his soup. Tell his other loving daughters it's safe to come back.

[GAIL *leaves.* NORA *goes to the basement door*]

NORA Mary Ann. You can come up now. [*she goes to the screen door*] Elizabeth. It's all right. He's upstairs. [*she goes to the table. Sits. Pours herself some tea*] Mary Ann! ... Elizabeth! [*A moment's pause. From the basement,* MARY ANN *appears. Behind her, with a hand over* MARY ANN*'s mouth, is*

40

STEVIE MOORE. *He is holding a gun*]

STEVIE Okay, lady. Stay real calm. Stay calm, and I don't hurt
her.

[*He takes* MARY ANN *to the screen door. Yells out*]

You out there? Okay. Come in ... Come on, come on. [*to*
NORA] Okay, stay calm.

[*The screen door opens.* ELIZABETH *appears. Behind her is*
ROLLY MOORE. *He has his arm around her throat. A gun to
her head*]

ROLLY Did you tell everyone to stay calm.

STEVIE Yeah.

ROLLY Are they. Are they calm.

[MARY ANN *passes out in* STEVIE'*s arms*]

STEVIE I don't know for sure. But I think so. I think they're
calm. Look at them ... What do you think.

[STEVIE *lays* MARY ANN *against a cupboard*]

ROLLY Yeah. I guess. Okay. [*to* NORA] You're the mother,
right. We know you. [*to* STEVIE] Did you tell her the thing.

STEVIE Yeah ... No.

[ROLLY *cuffs* STEVIE]

ROLLY [*to* NORA] Okay, this is the thing. You've got something
of ours. We want it back. That's the thing.

STEVIE The thing is, also, we're ready to kill.

ROLLY Yeah. That's part of the thing, too. We're ready to kill.
You understand us so far.

NORA Yes.

ROLLY Okay. So far so good. [*to* STEVIE] What do you say.

STEVIE Yeah. I say that, too. So far so good.

ROLLY Okay.

[STEVIE *and* ROLLY *look at each other. Nod.* GAIL *comes in,
breast-feeding the baby who is wrapped in a blanket. A long
pause*]

GAIL Great. Just great.

STEVIE Oh, man. Dad, she's got a baby.

ROLLY I can see that.

STEVIE I can't do bad things to a baby. No way.

ROLLY Yeah. Okay. No one ever asked you to hurt a baby. Stay calm. Everyone! Stay calm.

GAIL I know you guys. You're the guys who put my husband in the hospital.

NORA Gail. We don't have any opinion about the identity of these two men. These two men could leave now, and it would be like they were never here.

ROLLY Except we need something you've got. And the thing is—the thing is—

STEVIE I can't, Dad. Not in front of a baby. We might have to use maximum force here. And I don't know. I just don't know.

ROLLY Hey, stay relaxed. You know. Calm down. Okay. Okay. This is the thing ... We're ... leaving. [*to* NORA] Like you said. We were never here.

STEVIE Yeah. We were never here. But we'll be back.

ROLLY We'll have to come back. Because the thing you've got, we need it. I don't know. Maybe you don't even know you've got it. It's a ... strange thing.

STEVIE Yeah. But we can't get into that now.

ROLLY Right. Now we're leaving.

[*They look at each other. Nod. Back up. Go out the screen door.* ELIZABETH *goes to the sink. Fills a glass with water*]

GAIL Did you see that. Those assholes had guns. Didn't I tell you. This is a serious situation we've got here. Maybe next time I call a family meeting to discuss this situation we can stick to the fucking point!

[ELIZABETH *walks past* MARY ANN *without stopping. She throws the water in* MARY ANN*'s face.* MARY ANN *wakes up suddenly.* ELIZABETH *continues to the telephone. Picks up the receiver*]

GAIL What are you doing.

ELIZABETH Calling the police.

GAIL No.

MARY ANN Yes.

GAIL No!

ELIZABETH Yes!

GAIL Mom?

NORA I have mixed feelings. Give me a minute to think about it.
[*They are all looking at her.* GAIL *hands the baby to*
MARY ANN]

GAIL Mom, we don't need the police. They're all pricks. I
don't trust them. No fucking way do I trust them. We can
handle this ourselves. If we just put our heads together, and
forget all that other shit, and try to concentrate on this one
fucking problem here, we can do it on our own. We can,
Mom! Goddammit!

NORA Just a minute. I'm thinking. In the meantime, Gail, if
you don't mind me giving you a bit of advice. I think now
that you're a young mother with an innocent child you
should try to watch your language. Every time we run into
a bit of trouble your language deteriorates and eventually
winds up in the gutter. It's not the words themselves that
bother me. But they show that in some way you've given
up. That you feel trapped. Had a failure of the imagination. And that's not the state of mind a young mother
should be in. A young mother should be positive at all
costs. No matter what the world throws in your direction,
you should remain positive, remain buoyant, light … light
as a feather. In fact, that's good advice for all of you.
Remain light as feathers and everything will be fine.
[*Pause*]

GAIL [*looks at* ELIZABETH. *Gestures feebly*] You better call the
police.

ELIZABETH Okay.
[ELIZABETH *is dialling.* MARY ANN *is trying to get the baby's
attention, making little noises for her.* NORA *is looking around
at all her daughters. Smiling.* GAIL *is shaking her head, sadly*]
[*Blackout*]

Scene Three

DIAN *and* MARY ANN
DIAN *is sitting at the table, nibbling on a sandwich* MARY ANN *has made for her*
MARY ANN *is busy icing a chocolate cake and occasionally rearranging the condiments in front of* DIAN

MARY ANN Is this family doomed. I used to ask myself that question all the time. Are we forever doomed. Forever on the brink of destruction. Under some enormous shadow. Has God constructed a gigantic, mean-spirited shadow full of noxious, evil vibrations emanating poisonous, soul-killing rays, that has one job and one job only. To hover over this family and keep us doomed. And then one day I asked myself, why would God single out this family. And I knew right away that God wouldn't. God just made the shadow. And like everything else that God made, the shadow has a mind of its own. The shadow picked this family to hover over. I figured all this out a while ago, and it came as a great relief. You see, I didn't have to wonder anymore how we'd displeased God. I could forget about God for a while—which is always a great relief for me, seeing how I feel basically that God hates me— Mustard?
DIAN No thanks.
MARY ANN Anyway, I could forget about God, and concentrate on the shadow, and what possibly motivated it. You see, the shadow is fate. And our fate, the fate of this family, has some enormous grudge against us. So I figure we have to appease it, make amends, make some kind of huge, almost mythic, apology. We have to find a way of apologizing for something we don't know we did. So it has to be symbolic. It has to symbolize in some way everything bad each one of us has ever done as an individual or as part of a group. It's an almost impossible task. But we have to do it soon.

Because we're doomed. Unless we make the shadow, you know, go away. Events are unfolding here that prove we're running out of time. Right now I'm making a chocolate cake, but inside what I'm really doing is apologizing. This cake is an apology for all the times I know that people I loved or people I hardly knew needed some special little treat, and I didn't have the energy to make them one. Just a little thing. But you see this huge, symbolic apology will actually be made from thousands and thousands of little things just like this ... This cake ... This chocolate cake, and oatmeal cookies, and blueberry pancakes, fudge, a nicely pressed pair of slacks, a bit of change to someone in need, taking care of a friend's cat, smiling on the subway. These are the things that are going to save this family.

DIAN You're an awful lot like your mother. I guess people have told you that before.

MARY ANN A chip off the old block. Yeah. Sort of. What do you mean!

[NORA *comes in from upstairs*]

NORA [*to* DIAN] Your partner said to tell you he'll be right down. He searched the entire upstairs. He has a search warrant.

DIAN Yes, I know.

NORA Right now he's in that man's room. Talking. He thinks he knows him, of course. Just like everyone else around here. What can I do about it.

MARY ANN Bake a cake. Fix a chair. Give someone a hug. The little things.

NORA That's right, dear. The little things.

[*They hug each other*]

Did you call your daughter yet, Mary Ann.

MARY ANN Yes, Mom. She's fine. She misses me.

NORA Maybe you should go see her. I'm sure she misses you. But it's also possible she's beginning to question your reliability.

MARY ANN That's a chance I'll have to take.

[MIKE *comes in, laughing*]

MIKE Same old Tom. The same basic guy. Still breaks me up. Don't know why ... [*to* DIAN] Upstairs is clear.

DIAN What about the basement.

MIKE I know, the basement. [*to* NORA] Where's the basement.

[NORA *points*]

I suppose you want to come with me. [*laughs*] You know, to make sure I don't plant anything.

NORA If it's all right.

DIAN Go ahead.

MIKE Are you giving her permission. I was talking to her. But *you're* giving her permission.

DIAN She doesn't actually need permission.

MIKE You're saying that? You're saying that in front of *her?* Okay. If you say so.

DIAN I do.

MIKE [*to* NORA] Come on. To the basement.

[MIKE *goes downstairs.* NORA *waves at* DIAN. *Goes downstairs*]

MARY ANN Would you like a piece of chocolate cake.

DIAN No, thank you. Would you mind answering a few questions for me.

MARY ANN I don't like questions. I'd rather just give you things. If you don't want any cake, maybe I could make you another sandwich ... or a casserole ...

DIAN They're not hard questions. I'm just looking for a little clarification.

MARY ANN Oh my God. Clarification. I'm no good at that at all. Maybe in a year or two. Right now I'm just working on saying anything that comes into my mind. You know, unblocking myself. Maybe you could wait till my sister Elizabeth gets here. She's an expert on clarification. It's almost an obsession with her.

DIAN Elizabeth. She's the lawyer?

MARY ANN Yes. A lesbian lawyer. We're very proud of her. She overcame so much to be what she is. Well, look around. This family has nothing. We used to have a bit. The usual amount a family like ours has. But our father took it all away when he left. Of course he came back eventually, but he didn't bring anything with him. Except some strange ideas about the world … And now, well, he's a vegetable, sort of. That's what they tell me. I don't know for sure, though, because I never see him. He scares me. It's odd about my father. Because we're all reasonably intelligent. Had fairly good educations. Decent prospects. But when he deserted us, everything just fell apart. Who would have thought he had that kind of power. Not me. Before he deserted us, I barely gave him a second thought … Except when he was doing something loud and horrible. But we were talking about Elizabeth … Why? Why were we talking about Elizabeth.

DIAN Elizabeth seems to be a very important part of this family.

MARY ANN She's our weapon. She's the thing that protects us. I mean, if we're threatened.

DIAN Like now.

MARY ANN Like now. And then. Whenever.

DIAN She must care about you all very much. That's a heavy responsibility to take on.

MARY ANN She can handle it.

DIAN Mary Ann. Here's the problem I have. The men who broke in here, the men who beat up Junior … Your mother seems to know these men …

MARY ANN That's actually a question, isn't it. I'm supposed to answer that, I can tell.

DIAN Just try to make that clear for me. We won't dwell on it. And then maybe I'll have a piece of cake or something.

MARY ANN Okay. My mother hires people. Men mostly. Derelicts. Fallen men. Criminals even. She hires them to do handiwork around the house. She just finds them, we don't know how. They come here and work. She talks to them. Pays them. Talks to them some more.

DIAN Talks about what. I mean generally.

MARY ANN Life, I think. Gail says—Gail is my younger sister—

DIAN I know.

MARY ANN Gail says she's trying to reform them. Gail says it's ... bullshit. Elizabeth doesn't have an opinion about it. Elizabeth respects our mother a lot. She doesn't question anything she does. Sometimes that's good. Sometimes *that's* bullshit. I mean, Mom needs guidance as much as ... Anyway, these two men were probably men she hired once. Men she talked to about life.

DIAN So she wouldn't really know much about them. She wouldn't know their names, or ... how to find them ...

MARY ANN No. She doesn't ask them questions like that. She doesn't ask them anything, really. She just talks to them. Would you like that cake now.

DIAN Sure. You know, Mary Ann, this is one rough neighbourhood here. The crime statistics for this area are appalling. This is a dangerous world you live in. If you'll take a little advice, perhaps your family should try a more realistic approach in dealing with it.

MARY ANN [*cuts a piece of cake. Puts it on a plate*] Realistic? Oh. I think I know what you mean. We've tried that. It doesn't seem to work for us. It was very real when I was a kid. My dad was here. There was anger and violence. Hopelessness. I think what we do now is better. It's more like Mom than Dad. And Mom's way is more ... well, more ...

DIAN Innocent.

MARY ANN No. [*laughs*] Innocent? No ... Hopeful.

[NORA *comes up*]

NORA He found something. I'm a little worried.

[MIKE *comes up. Carrying two large garbage bags. Each about half full*]

49

MIKE [*to* DIAN] They were hidden in a hole in the wall. Behind a work bench.

[MIKE *puts the bags down.* DIAN *goes over. Looks in them*]

DIAN Did you know about these bags, Nora.

NORA No.

DIAN So you don't know what's in them.

NORA No. I mean, I suspect it's something of substance. Some substantially evil thing. I picked that up from the substantially evil way your partner smiled at me.

MIKE Hey!

NORA [*to* MARY ANN] I'm a little worried about the neighbourhood fanatics. What are they making of all this. Break-ins. Police cars. I bet they're passing around a petition at this very moment.

DIAN Drugs.

MARY ANN Oh my God.

[MARY ANN *goes to* NORA. *Puts her arms around her neck. Hangs on*]

DIAN Hundreds of thousands of dollars worth of drugs. I think you'll have to come with us, Nora, so we can straighten this out. I'm sorry.

MIKE You're sorry. You're telling her you're sorry.

DIAN That's right. Come on, she didn't know they were there.

MIKE [*goes to* DIAN] You're saying that. You're saying that right in front of her. Where the fuck were you trained. Disneyland?

DIAN I'll deal with you later!

MIKE I'll deal with *you* later! [*to* NORA] Turn around. Put your hands behind your back.

[MIKE *is trying to handcuff* NORA. *But* MARY ANN *still has her arms around* NORA *and is turning her around.* MIKE *is turning with them*]

DIAN No cuffs.

[DIAN *is trying to restrain* MIKE]

MIKE I've got contraband here. I've got hard evidence right fucking here. And this is *the* suspect. We're in a war here. You ever hear about it. It's called the war on drugs. Drugs are the main thing now. It's what we're all about. It's our reason for fucking living, and she's a suspected drug dealer. [*All four of them are tangled and turning*]

DIAN No fucking cuffs! And get your hands off her! If you don't get your hands off her right now I'll have your head! [DIAN *groans and pulls* MIKE *away from* NORA *and* MARY ANN. *She is poking him in the chest and backing him up.* MIKE *is trying to resist. Trying to control his temper*] I've got friends. Friends high up. [*poke*]

MIKE Back off.

DIAN You know, the ones you resent. The ones you talk about behind my back. [*poke*]

MIKE Get your hands off me. Back off.

DIAN The ones you say gave me my job because I screwed their brains out. [*poke*]

MIKE Back off. I'm warning you.

DIAN I think you should assume these friends will do anything for me! [*poke*]

MIKE Hey, you were warned. Now back the fuck off! [*He pokes her. She grabs him by the collar. He grabs her by the collar*]

DIAN If I ask them, my friends will take your badge and shove it so far up your ass your spleen will think it's under arrest!!

MIKE You talk to me like that?! In front of them?! I gotta say fuck you! I really do! [*he shakes himself free. To* DIAN] Fuck you. [*to* NORA *and* MARY ANN] Fuck you, too. [*he picks up the garbage bags. To* NORA *and* MARY ANN] No, to you I'm sorry. [*to* DIAN] But to you, definitely, fuck you! [*He leaves.*]

DIAN [*is trembling slightly. She searches her purse. Finds a small plastic tube*] Lip balm. Do you mind.

NORA No.

DIAN [*applies the lip balm, strenuously*] That was ugly, wasn't it.

Sorry you had to witness that. Obviously my partner and I are having problems maintaining a relationship. There are just so many co-factors involved. So many differences. Age, sex, levels of intelligence. The conflicts are very deep. The relationship is deteriorating rapidly.

NORA Would you like a cup of tea, dear.

DIAN No.

MARY ANN Cake?

DIAN No. Thank you … We should go now, Nora. We'll just go back to the office. Meet my supervisor. Talk this thing through in detail. You'll be back in no time.

MARY ANN I want to come, too.

NORA No you don't, dear.

MARY ANN You're right. I *want* to want to come. But I don't really want to come at all.

NORA And you don't have to. So why bother. [*to* DIAN] Right?

DIAN [*to* MARY ANN] She won't be long. [*to* NORA] Do you need a coat … or a sweater.

NORA No … Should I call my daughter Elizabeth, though. She's a lawyer.

MARY ANN She's the lesbian, remember. You'd like her. Not that I think you're a lesbian. Not that there's anything wrong with being a lesbian. I'm thinking about it myself. I just meant she was … well, you know what I meant.

DIAN No. But it's all right. Come on, Nora. You can call Elizabeth from my office, if you feel it's necessary.

NORA [*goes to* MARY ANN] Maybe you could cook supper.

MARY ANN I would anyway. That's what I do when I run away from home, remember. I come here and cook things.

NORA I've been thinking, Mary Ann. It's possible you aren't a good mother. It's possible you're just average. Maybe you could go home and just be a good, average mother. Maybe that would be enough. Think about that while you're cooking. I'll see you soon.

[NORA *and* DIAN *leave.* MARY ANN *looks around. Lost. She*

52

goes to the table. Sits in a chair. Puts her head in her palms.]

MARY ANN [*looks up suddenly, a puzzled look on her face*] When
I said she'd like Elizabeth because Elizabeth is a lesbian what
did I mean. Really. I think I meant Elizabeth is great. She'd like
her because she's great. Why do I say lesbian instead of great ...
I don't know. But maybe I don't really want to be a lesbian.
Maybe I just want to be ... great ... Do I have to be a lesbian
to be great ... I'll ask Elizabeth. She wasn't always a lesbian.
She wasn't always great, either. What came first. The lesbian-
ism or the greatness. When did she become lesbianistic. Is that
a word? Use it in a sentence. Never mind. It's beside the point.
Just ask her. Okay. Yeah. Of course, she hardly ever listens to
me, so it'll be hard. Unless I cry. When I cry she listens. Okay.
Yeah. I'll cry. It's demeaning. But I'll do it. Because I need to
know. I mean, I'm working things out here. Important things.
Yeah.

[TOM *appears at the hallway door*]

TOM I'm starving to death.

MARY ANN Oh dear.

[*She stands. Hurries towards the basement door. Leaves.
Reappears*]

No. No. I can do better than this. I can. [*looks at* TOM.
Smiles weakly] Hi.

TOM Hi.

MARY ANN You're hungry?

TOM [*lowers his head*] I'm starving to death.

MARY ANN Would you like some chocolate cake.

TOM Not soup?

MARY ANN I can do soup. Soup is all right, too. I'll ... make
you some. From scratch. I'm good at soups. It'll take some
time. Can you wait.

TOM No.

MARY ANN Okay. Have the cake now. Here. I'll cut you a
piece. No. Here, take it all. Here's a fork. Take it.

TOM [*he takes the cake*] It's big.

MARY ANN Yeah.

TOM But there's a piece missing.

MARY ANN Is that okay.

TOM I don't know. Why shouldn't it be. Can you think of a reason. Who are you, anyway.

MARY ANN Mary Ann.

TOM My daughter?

MARY ANN Yeah.

TOM I've got to ask you a question.

MARY ANN Oh ... okay ... I guess.

TOM How you doin'. How's your life. Are you having a good life. Have you recovered.

MARY ANN Ah ... From what.

TOM Me ... I guess. Recovered from me. The things I did. I did some bad things to this family. I think I had a ... I had a, I had a—

MARY ANN Problem. You had a problem.

TOM Drinking.

MARY ANN Drinking. Yeah. And a vicious temper. And awful impatience. But, well ... I'm okay. Sure, I'm fine now. That was your question? So ... I'm basically ... well, I've got some things to work on ... some choices I have to ... but basically—

TOM I'm tired.

[*He leaves.* MARY ANN *sits down. Lowers her head on to the table. Keeps it there a moment. Sits up*]

MARY ANN Soup.

[*She stands. Goes to the cupboard, the fridge. Hunting up ingredients for vegetable soup.* GAIL *and* JUNIOR *come in through the screen door.* GAIL *is helping* JUNIOR, *who has a slight limp, an arm in a cast and sling, and various cuts and bruises on his face.* ELIZABETH *is right behind them carrying a small suitcase*]

GAIL Hi ... Well, here he is. Look at him. Disgusting, isn't it. If I get my hands on those creeps I'm going to rip their faces off.

ELIZABETH What good will that do. [*she heads for the telephone. Punches in her code. Takes out a pad*]

GAIL It will make me feel terrific. That's what. You know, sometimes you just have to lash out, Elizabeth. You just have to lash out to keep yourself from going nuts. I learned that from you, Elizabeth. That's how you used to be before you became so … busy.

ELIZABETH What's your problem. You've been sniping at me all day. You were taking shots all the way home in the car.

JUNIOR Can I sit down.

MARY ANN Let me help you.

JUNIOR Hi, Mary Ann. Why are you looking at me like that. I look pretty bad, eh.

MARY ANN You probably just need some food. [*she makes herself busy*] Lots and lots of food.

GAIL [*to* ELIZABETH] You had your chance with those guys. You had them right here in your grasp, and you didn't do anything to them. That pisses me off.

ELIZABETH They had guns.

GAIL So what. That wouldn't have stopped you before. You'd have taken their guns and made them eat them.

ELIZABETH You think so?

GAIL No doubt. Before you got busy you were tough. We relied on you. [*to* MARY ANN] Didn't we.

MARY ANN Yes. She was great. Well, not always. But at some point she got great. She's still great. But we just can't rely on her, that's all.

JUNIOR Could I have a glass of water.

GAIL Sure, honey. I'll get it.

MARY ANN I'll get it.

GAIL I said I'd get it!

ELIZABETH You're too much. Both of you. If you thought I was so great before why didn't you tell me. All you ever did was complain that I was bossing you around.

GAIL So what. That shouldn't have bothered you. You should have just continued to be tough. If you were really tough you would have just ignored us. It really pisses me off. This change in you. Especially now. Look at Junior. Pathetic or what. He's probably going to lose his job, too.

JUNIOR Ah, no. You think so?

GAIL Your foreman called. He said the police were by the plant. They told him some bad stuff about you. I'm going to go talk to him later. Maybe I can fix it.

JUNIOR Maybe I should talk to him.

GAIL Yeah? What would you say.

JUNIOR Ah, I don't really—

GAIL Well, until you can think of something, leave it to me. [*to* MARY ANN] Where's my baby.

MARY ANN Still asleep, I think.

GAIL What do you mean you think. Haven't you been checking on her.

MARY ANN I checked her a while ago.

GAIL When.

MARY ANN I don't know.

GAIL Well, was it ten minutes, an hour, two hours.

MARY ANN I don't know!

GAIL Too much. I feel like I'm in one of those science fiction movies where I'm the only human being, and everyone else is some kind of plant life.

MARY ANN I feel that way sometimes, too. Only the opposite.

GAIL There. That's an example of what I mean. Nothing you say makes any sense to me. In fact nothing makes much sense to me these days. I'm married to a guy who has bad luck following him around like it's a close friend. And my oldest sister here, who I used to trust more than anyone, has turned out to be the biggest disappointment in my life. [GAIL *grabs the phone from* ELIZABETH. *Hangs up*]

ELIZABETH Ah, come off it. I'm not responsible for all your problems. Where the hell do you get off blaming me.

GAIL I'm not blaming you for the problems, Elizabeth. I'm blaming you for not helping to solve them. Are you a member of this family or not.

MARY ANN She's changed, Gail. She's a changed person and she's trying to deal with it. It's because she's—

ELIZABETH If you say I'm a lesbian again I'm going to take you upstairs and drown you in the bathtub.

MARY ANN Are you saying you're *not* a lesbian.

ELIZABETH Who I sleep with isn't the issue. It's never the issue. It's always never the issue. Why are you trying to make it so important. I sleep with women *and* men, if you must know. I sleep with anyone I like. I find nice, sexy people and I sleep with them.

GAIL When you can spare the time.

ELIZABETH Ah, fuck off.

GAIL Go ahead. Talk some more about yourself. Talk about your personal life, your love life. Like it's some big deal. Like we really care. I've got to go check on my baby. [*She leaves*]

ELIZABETH Unbelievable. Why is she on my back like this. What the hell is her problem.

JUNIOR She's upset.

ELIZABETH I'm upset.

MARY ANN I'm upset, too! You were supposed to be a lesbian. You were supposed to have made a choice. But no. You sleep with anyone just because they're nice! What kind of choice is that. That's not courageous. That's not politically … important. Anyone can do that. Even I can do that.

ELIZABETH No! No you can't. You can't even sleep with your husband. So go to hell!

MARY ANN Don't talk to me! I'm busy. I'm cooking. And I'm re-examining my life! [*she is cutting vegetables*]

JUNIOR Where's Mom.

MARY ANN At the police station.

ELIZABETH What's she doing there.

MARY ANN The police took her there.

ELIZABETH Why?

JUNIOR Is she under arrest.

MARY ANN I don't think so.

ELIZABETH [*to* JUNIOR] Get serious. She's not under arrest. [*to* MARY ANN] What do you mean you don't think so. You don't know for sure?

MARY ANN That's right. Not for sure.

ELIZABETH Could you make a guess.

MARY ANN No. Not really. They said they just wanted to question her. But that could have been a trick. Something they just said so she wouldn't make a fuss.

ELIZABETH They can't do that. If she was under arrest they'd have to tell her.

MARY ANN That's what you say about that now. Who knows what you'll say about it tomorrow. Maybe tomorrow you'll say they can arrest anyone anytime. Men. Women. Anyone who is sexy. And nice!

ELIZABETH Shut up!

JUNIOR Question her about what.

MARY ANN About what they found when they searched the house.

ELIZABETH They searched the house? You let them search the house?

MARY ANN They had a warrant. Mom said it looked official.

JUNIOR What did they find.

MARY ANN Drugs. In the basement.

ELIZABETH What are you talking about?!

MARY ANN Hundreds of thousands of dollars worth of drugs in two garbage bags.

[JUNIOR *groans. Puts his head down on the table*]

ELIZABETH How the hell did they get there.

MARY ANN How am I supposed to know. Questions I can answer are one thing. Questions like that I don't feel bad for ignoring.

ELIZABETH Oh God, you're too much, Mary Ann. And you didn't think any of this was worth mentioning when we first got here. Cops come here with a warrant, search our house, find a bag full of dope, take our mother away, and you just go about your business like usual. You just cook something!

MARY ANN Dad's hungry.

ELIZABETH *Who's hungry?*

MARY ANN Dad. I talked to him. Yes. I know we promised we never would, but I couldn't help it. I was trying to be a better person. Make apologies. Do little things.

ELIZABETH You're apologizing to him? You've got that kind of ass-backwards, haven't you.

MARY ANN Not in the mythic, larger—

ELIZABETH Shut up. We'll deal with that later. [*she starts off*] I'm going after Mom. She's probably scared half to death. [*stops*] Where'd they take her. To the local police station. Or downtown to headquarters. Why am I asking you that. You don't know, do you. You didn't fucking ask, did you. Did you?!

MARY ANN That's right! I didn't!! I'm sorry!

[ELIZABETH *grabs* MARY ANN]

ELIZABETH When I get back I'm going to do something to you, Mary Ann. I'm going to change your outlook on life. I'm going to crawl inside your brain and alter your entire personality. The neurotic idiot child you are now is going to cease to exist. Say goodbye to her forever! ... Shit!

[*She goes out the back.* JUNIOR *lifts his head*]

MARY ANN [*kind of thrilled*] That's how she used to talk to me. Remember?

JUNIOR Yeah.

MARY ANN You look worried.

JUNIOR Aren't you.

MARY ANN About Elizabeth? No. I like it sort of when she talks to me like that. It makes me feel comfortable, safe ...

I can't explain it. I'm sure it's not healthy, but what can I do.

JUNIOR I meant your mother. Aren't you worried about your mother being in jail.

MARY ANN Oh yeah. But I can't think about that. I'd die.

JUNIOR Really?

MARY ANN Oh yeah. I'd die. I'm not ready for that yet.

JUNIOR Oh.

MARY ANN Well, in four or five years maybe ...

[GAIL *comes back in*]

GAIL She was hungry. She was lying there ... hungry. [*to* JUNIOR] You know that sad, hurt little look she gets.

MARY ANN Why didn't she cry.

GAIL She doesn't cry.

MARY ANN Not even when she's hungry. Why not.

GAIL I don't know. Maybe she just trusts us. Maybe she thought, 'Hey, they're all responsible adults. One of them is bound to look in on me before I starve to death.'

MARY ANN Well, if I were you I'd teach her how to cry. Adults can let you down. They aren't perfect ... I think adults are expected to do too much, anyway. Why can't we—

GAIL Be quiet. Why do you do that. I was just being sarcastic. Just trying to make a point. Why can't you just let me make my point without launching into one of those long, complicated ... things. You're getting more like Mom every day.

MARY ANN I know.

GAIL In some ways. Just in some ways. I mean, Mom cares more about kids. Mom would never neglect a kid.

MARY ANN [*starts to cry*] I know! I know!

[*Pause*]

GAIL I looked in on Dad. He says you're making him soup. He's fantasizing, right.

MARY ANN No. I'm doing it.

GAIL Really ... He says you talked to him.

MARY ANN A little.

GAIL Really ... Do you want to talk to him some more? He needs company. I could finish the soup.

MARY ANN It's vegetable. Not out of a can. From scratch.

GAIL I think I can manage that, Mary Ann. Do you want to go up and see him.

MARY ANN I don't know. Maybe I said all I've got to say to him right now.

GAIL You could read to him. He likes that. There's a pile of books beside his bed ... So?

[*Pause.* MARY ANN *is staring at the floor*]

Come on, Mary Ann. What's it going to be. Are you going all the way with this one or not. Are we going to be living in the past forever with this guy, or are we going to make a little progress here. There's nothing to lose, Mary Ann. He's dying. Do it for the same reason I do it. So that when he's dead you won't feel so shitty. You'll feel it was basically okay with him for a while at least. Not great. But okay.

[*Pause*]

MARY ANN Yeah.

[*She leaves*]

GAIL That's a breakthrough. You know, just when you've written her off she surprises you. She's always done that. Sometimes at the last moment ... You know, just when your hands are around her throat, and you're about to apply serious pressure.

JUNIOR I like her. I've always liked her.

GAIL Because she likes you.

JUNIOR Yeah. Maybe.

GAIL What's wrong. That look on your face. Are you in pain.

JUNIOR Come here. Sit down. Here. On my lap.

GAIL What about your ribs.

JUNIOR Don't worry.

GAIL Nah. I don't want to hurt you, honey. I'll sit next to you.

[*she does*]

JUNIOR But you see, I'd kind of like to hold you ...

GAIL Are you going to cry.

JUNIOR No.

GAIL That's what you say when you're going to cry. That you want to hold me.

JUNIOR Yeah. I know. But I'm not. Just sit on my lap.

GAIL Okay. But let's be careful.

[*She sits on his lap. Puts her arm around him*]

What's wrong. Something real terrible I bet. You had another one of those dreams where I meet someone with money and style, and take off with him.

JUNIOR Your mother's in jail.

GAIL Oh. Right. Sure.

JUNIOR The cops found some drugs in the house. I guess they think she's been dealin'.

[GAIL *starts to laugh. Harder. Really hard. Rolls off* JUNIOR. *On to the floor. Sits up. Points at him*]

GAIL I love you. You always know when I need to laugh.

JUNIOR No, seriously. The drugs were in the basement. In green garbage bags. Hundreds of thousands of dollars worth.

[GAIL *pounds the floor. Laughing almost hysterically. Falling back*]

No, seriously … Gail … We've got a real problem here. Come on. Really.

[*Lights start to fade.* GAIL*'s laughter continues into the …*]
[*Blackout*]
[*Intermission*]

Scene Four

JUNIOR, MARY ANN *and* TOM *are at the table*
TOM *has a blanket around him, his head bowed.* JUNIOR *is
feeding* TOM *soup. He has to lift* TOM*'s head for each spoonful.*
MARY ANN *has her elbows on the table, her head in her hands.
She's staring at* TOM. *Smiling a little*
After a while, GAIL *comes in from the hallway, pushing the baby
in a stroller*

GAIL I'm off. I won't be long.

JUNIOR Where are you going.

GAIL I told you. To talk to your foreman.

JUNIOR You can leave the baby here, if you want.

GAIL Are you kidding. This beautiful, little girl is going to save
your job. I'm going to pick her up, put her eye level with
that foreman, and dare him to fire you. If that doesn't
work, I'll beg. Listen, I guess I should ask you. You don't
mind me doing this, do you. I mean, it won't make you
feel weak, or unmanly, or something stupid like that.

JUNIOR Just save my job. That's the only important thing.

GAIL I love you. Are you coming, Mary Ann.

MARY ANN Where are you going.

GAIL How do you do that, Mary Ann. How can you be in a
room and not hear a word that's said.

MARY ANN I don't know. Practice, I guess. Where are you
going.

GAIL I've got something to do. And then I thought we'd go
shopping.

MARY ANN Grocery shopping?

GAIL Whatever. Do you have any money.

MARY ANN Yeah. I took some of our life savings. Larry always
agrees to let me do that when I leave. You know, so I won't
be a burden to anyone.

GAIL Larry is a very generous, understanding man. Larry might be Jesus Christ come back to earth, did you ever think of that.

MARY ANN He's got faults like everyone else. For one thing, he hasn't had a new thought in twenty years. You see, Larry modelled himself on his father. And he had the finished product by the time he was twelve. So you can't make me feel bad saying things like that. I'm beyond guilt anyway. I'm in some other place now.

GAIL Yeah. Where is it.

MARY ANN [*shrugs*] It's in the place where I have to be.

GAIL Let's not talk to each other for a while. Let's just go shopping.

MARY ANN Okay. [*she stands*]

JUNIOR Was that Elizabeth again on the phone.

GAIL Yeah.

JUNIOR Something wrong? She got Mom away from those cops, didn't she. They didn't try to take her back or anything.

GAIL No, they're still letting her go for now. Elizabeth just wanted me to know they had something to do before they came home. She wouldn't tell me what. She sounded really, really ticked off. Like the old Elizabeth. It's great to hear her like that.

MARY ANN Yeah. It is, isn't it. I wonder why. Do you think we've got a hang-up about Elizabeth. You know, some older-sister-as-a-parent kind of thing.

GAIL Yeah. Probably. So what. Let's go. [*to* JUNIOR] See ya. [JUNIOR *waves*]

MARY ANN Because Elizabeth can be so firm. And Mom was never really firm. And Dad wasn't here. And …
[GAIL *opens the back door. Pushes* MARY ANN *through. Follows her.* JUNIOR *stands. Limps over to the door. Limps back*]

JUNIOR Great! The cops think someone is dealing dope out of this house. This house right here. People we're supposed to love are living in this house … Right here!

[TOM *mumbles*]

What? I can't hear you. Lift your head. They're gone.

TOM I'm afraid they might come back. If they come back and see me normal they'll make me leave. [*he lowers his head*]

JUNIOR They're not coming back. Lift your head. We have to talk. The people in this house are in deep trouble.

TOM [*lifts his head*] Yeah. I know. Did you put drugs in our basement ... for some reason.

JUNIOR No. I thought you did for some reason.

TOM Then it's a mistake. [*he lowers his head*]

JUNIOR A mistake? Someone's going to jail. In my bones I feel it. In my head I've got a picture of it. Someone in this house is going to do some time over this. Whatya mean a mistake. That's gotta be the wrong word. You gotta mean something else. Think about it. A mistake is like ... an accident. Those garbage bags didn't get down there by accident. Please lift your fucking head! I need your help!

TOM [*lifts his head*] I mean a mistake in our strategy. We left ourselves open somehow. Someone figured out what we were doing, and did it to us for some reason.

JUNIOR Who the hell could figure out what we were doing. I mean, I was actually doing it, and I could hardly understand it myself.

TOM Look, you have to stop underestimating these crooks. I warned you about that right from the start.

JUNIOR No you didn't. You just threw me in. Right into the middle of a bunch of low-life scum.

TOM They're scum. But they've got experience. Experience can make stupid people smart. Experience is a kind of replacement for intelligence.

JUNIOR Not close up. Not when they open their mouths and talk to you. You've put me in a position where I've had to listen to a lot of scum talking right at me. Real close, you know? Guys who mug, steal, break and enter. Guys who rent their sisters out for twelve dollars an hour. They

65

trusted me. They showed their, you know, inner thoughts. And their inner thoughts are stupid! So stupid they make me want to puke. God, man. They're everywhere. And I'm right in the middle of them.

TOM [*pulls himself closer to the table*] That's right! That's my point, goddammit! This neighbourhood is going down the toilet. And no one else seems to be doing anything about it. Fucking cops, social workers, fucking press. Bastards. Maybe they think it's hopeless. Rotten bastards! I don't know ... Maybe they don't have enough at stake. Rotten, rotten bastards. But this is where my family lives. They can't afford to move. I owe it to them to fix their neighbourhood. Okay. Let's get to work! [*he stands suddenly*]

JUNIOR What? Calm down. Sit down. We're not doing anything. Not until we figure out what we've already done.

TOM I owe my family. You know I owe them! [*he is agitated. Moving around*]

JUNIOR Yeah. I know. But that's not—

[TOM *approaches* JUNIOR *quickly*]

TOM Do you! Do you really know?!

[TOM *grabs* JUNIOR *by the shoulder of his broken arm.*]

JUNIOR [*groans*] Yeah. I really do. I do!

TOM I hurt this family. I was a frigging monster. I have to make amends for all the bad things I did to them. I have to apologize in a really major way!

[TOM *is staring into space. Squeezing* JUNIOR'*s shoulder*]

JUNIOR Don't get too worked up, man.

TOM You know something? Do you want to know something I did? I tried to burn this house down once. I tried to burn it down while they were all asleep in their beds ... So I guess I tried to kill them. What do you think. Does that sound like attempted murder. Attempted goddamn mass murder!

JUNIOR Yeah. But try to calm down a little.

TOM They didn't even have me arrested. Nora felt sorry for me. God, man. What a lucky bastard I was. I owe them.

I've got to fix this part of the world where they live. This little part of the world is theirs. I've got to make it better. Really I do!

[TOM *starts to move around again.* JUNIOR *stands. Gently approaches* TOM]

JUNIOR Maybe you don't. Maybe it's too much. Maybe there's a limit to what you can do, you know, a line ... and you've crossed it. I've been thinking about this. Maybe you just have to talk to them. Let them see that you're basically all right now. Just be yourself.

[TOM *turns on* JUNIOR]

TOM Myself?! That's not enough!

[*He grabs* JUNIOR]

You know that! That's not enough. Goddammit!

[JUNIOR *loses his balance. Falls. Groans loudly. Grabs his broken arm*]

Ah, shit! I'm sorry. Are you all right.

JUNIOR Holy fuck. I can't believe what's happening to my life.

TOM I'm sorry ... You see, I can't be myself. This is the self I can't be. They'd never trust me. And who could blame them. If they knew I wasn't really sick and helpless they'd toss me out in a minute. [*he sits. Puts the blanket around himself*] I'm here because I don't look threatening to them. It has to stay that way. [*he lowers his head*]

JUNIOR [*getting up slowly*] So that's it? You've only got two speeds? You're either gonna rant and rave or sit there like a zombie. Can't we get you somewhere in between those two things. And can't we get you out of the past. Sort of here and now. And sort of normal. Because these people here are in deep shit right *now*. That's what I'm here trying to tell you. That's the real thing you've got to come to grips with here. Not that other stuff. The house thing. The drinking. That's yesterday's shit. Today we're in this new shit. I mean, come on, I'm probably going to lose my job. I'm the only person in this house with a real job. Mom still stuffs envelopes, but there's no real money there. She won't take anything from Elizabeth. Why? I don't know. She's got her reasons, and her reasons are always good in the long run, I guess. But now, well ... what'll we do. And there's the baby now, and Mary Ann's here. Probably for good this time. I figure her husband won't let her go back. I don't think he likes her much, anyway. I think he just liked her cooking. Which is a plus for us. I mean, if she concentrates on it, and doesn't leave out important ingredients, her cooking can be really good. And she hardly eats anything herself. So, overall Mary Ann is a plus. But it's still dire. Overall, it's a really dire thing we're in—and—and—

TOM Look, I'm sorry to interrupt. But what the fuck are you talking about. What's Mary Ann's cooking got to do with this. I thought you wanted to work out a solution here. This is no time to go haywire. You can't let your mind run around in circles like that.

[JUNIOR *puts his head down on the table*]

Okay. You're upset. We're both upset. And scared. Being scared is a hard thing for a, you know ... a man to admit. Okay, maybe not for you. But for me it is. Okay, this drug thing has caught us both off guard. Let's just say we're not at our best. Emotionally, I mean. Just the fact that we're behaving emotionally shows that we're not emotionally at our best. I'm speaking strictly as a ... you know, now. I know that can be ugly, but I can't help it. As ... *men* we expect certain things of ourselves, and right now we're in a state of bewilderment over our failures. But we're sharing that. We're going through that together. Each in our own way. And that's good.

JUNIOR [*looks up*] It is?

TOM It's gotta be. It means we're on the same track, basically. It means we both really want to help these people. But we're desperate. I think we need to relax a bit. So we can regroup. It's the pressure. A ... *man* has all this pressure to

68

prove things. So he gets worked up. It's the pressure of self-imposed leadership. Okay, it's bullshit. But it's genetic.

JUNIOR Someone's coming.

[*Noises outside*]

TOM Meet me here tonight. When they're all asleep. Together we'll work out a plan to save these people.

JUNIOR Okay. But it's got to be a plan that makes sense. Something I can understand.

TOM And something that won't put too much pressure on us.

[TOM *lowers his head.* JUNIOR *lowers his head, too.* NORA *and* ELIZABETH *come in. They are pushing a shopping cart, with something large inside it, covered with a blanket*]

ELIZABETH What's he doing down here. Tell him to go away.

JUNIOR He was just leaving. Tom ... Go ... upstairs. Upstairs, Tom. I'll bring your soup up in a minute.

[TOM *nods, rises slowly, leaves*]

[*to* ELIZABETH] I'm sorry about that. I was just ... I mean he ... asked me to ... tell him a story.

NORA Really. What kind of story. A war story?

JUNIOR No. Just a story ... I made one up. I did my best. I'm not very good at that stuff.

NORA You've become such a kind young man, Junior. I think about you sometimes, and how kind you've become, and it seems like a little miracle. Don't trust that man too much, though. Just because he's dying doesn't make him a good person.

JUNIOR What's in the cart.

ELIZABETH I decided to go on the offensive.

[ELIZABETH *pulls the blanket away. She and* NORA *tip the cart and* ROLLY *falls out on to the floor.* ROLLY's *feet and hands are bound. And he has an old rag stuffed in his mouth*]

You should recognize this man, Junior. He's one of the guys who beat you up.

JUNIOR [*stands*] Excuse me. I've got to go to the bathroom.

[*He leaves*]

NORA Was that an unusual response for Junior to have, Elizabeth.

ELIZABETH Probably not. Junior's a victim. Seeing his assailant again can't be the easiest thing in the world. Help me get this guy in a chair.

[*They are getting* ROLLY *settled in a chair*]

Okay, asshole. We're going to make you comfortable. Then I'm going to ungag you and ask you a few questions. The same questions I asked you in that alley. If you answer them this time I won't have to use this again. [*she has a can of mace strung around her neck*]

NORA [*to* ROLLY] Please don't make her use that ... that ... What's it called again, Elizabeth.

ELIZABETH It's mace, Mom.

NORA Please don't make her use the mace again, Mister. It was so upsetting to watch you writhe around like that. I can't think of any good reason to put us all through that again.

ELIZABETH Don't worry, Mom. He's going to be a good little asshole this time, aren't you fuck-face.

NORA You're the expert on these things, Elizabeth. I mean, your law practice and all. The people you meet there. But do you really think calling him names like that is helpful.

ELIZABETH It helps me, Mom. It makes me feel good. Don't worry. I'm sure he's been called worse. Right, ass-wipe?

[ROLLY *nods.* ELIZABETH *takes some rope from her pocket. Ties* ROLLY *to the chair*]

Good little asshole. Here, let me take this piss-soaked rag away from your mouth. How did such a disgusting, piss-soaked rag come to be the only thing in the vicinity suitable for sticking in your mouth. Well that's life, eh. That's what some of my friends might call karma. Karma can be a really ugly experience for dirt-bags like you ... There. Feel better?

[ROLLY *is making gagging sounds. Wiping his lips with his tongue. Groaning*]

NORA Can I take that rag away, Elizabeth. Or will you be needing it later.

ELIZABETH Depends. Just leave it on the floor for now … [*to* ROLLY] Okay, stay calm! [*smiles*] Are you ready for that first question, shit-head.

ROLLY Yeah.

ELIZABETH What's your name.

ROLLY Rolly. Rolly Moore.

ELIZABETH You're a crook, aren't you, Rolly.

ROLLY Whatya mean.

ELIZABETH You found that question difficult to understand?

ROLLY Come on. You ask if I'm a crook. What am I supposed to say. Yeah? What good can come to me for saying yeah to a question like that.

ELIZABETH I have to know who you are, Rolly. What you're up to. So I'm asking about how you make your living. You make your living by breaking the law. Right?

ROLLY Sometimes.

ELIZABETH Sometimes. So what are you saying here, Rolly. You occasionally do straight work.

ROLLY I'm not a young man. I can't always take the tension of doing crime. I need calmer things to do every once in a while. Ask her. I worked for her once.

NORA Yes. He helped me make my garden.

ROLLY I carried rocks. It was hard. But I didn't complain.

NORA Yes. You did. You complained a lot. And I think you stole my wheelbarrow.

ROLLY Come on. Hey. [*to* ELIZABETH] Is that what this is about. Jesus, you people gotta be kidding—a wheelbarrow. What's that cost, twenty bucks, I mean—

ELIZABETH Hey! Look at me. Take a good look at me. I'm a busy woman. If I have to keep listening to your bullshit you're going to get hurt!

ROLLY She brought it up. She was the one who brought up the thing about the wheelbarrow.

NORA That's true, Elizabeth. I did. [*to* ROLLY] She's upset. I'll tell you why. She believes the police are making plans to charge me with a very serious crime.

ROLLY That's too bad.

ELIZABETH All right! All right. Mom, why don't you go see how Junior's doing.

ROLLY Why does she have to leave. I'm a little nervous to be left alone with you. I'm sorry to offend you. But I'd feel a lot better if she stayed.

NORA Is that good, Elizabeth. Is it good or bad if he feels less nervous. You're the expert.

ELIZABETH Go ahead, Mom. We'll be fine.

NORA Please, Elizabeth. Just don't do anything you can't live with later.

[*She leaves.*]

ELIZABETH [*looks at* ROLLY. *Smiles*] I can live with a lot. By most people's standards that is. An awful lot. [*she leans into him. Close*] Now, you're probably going to try to dance around this for a while. Buy some time to help your little brain find its way out of this mess. I'm a very, very busy woman. I've got a law practice to keep going, and an apartment I've been trying to finish painting for six months. But I'm going to have to stay here and listen to some extreme amounts of bullshit from you unless we find a way to cut right to the issue here … Now, where's that piss-soaked rag. Ah, there it is.

[ELIZABETH *picks up the rag. Sprays it with mace. Grabs* ROLLY'*s nose, and when he opens his mouth, she shoves the rag in.* ROLLY *gags*]

Believe it or not, a part of me hates doing this to you. You're a pathetic bastard. I see guys like you every day. Messed up. Stupid. Defenceless. Beaten up by everything and everyone. You even get beaten up by the police. And that pisses me off. I'm truly pissed off that the police beat up pathetic bastards like you. They have no right, no right at all to punish you physically ... But this is different. I'm not the police. I'm not a representative of the state. I'm just a member of a family. A family you've fucked with! You see, this is personal. This is a deeply personal thing. This is not sanctioned by the government. And therefore there's a limit, a restriction on the damage that can be done here. The only thing that can be damaged here is you. And basically, I think that's okay. I'm not enjoying your suffering or anything. But it doesn't really bother me, because really, all I'm doing is ... defending my family.

[ELIZABETH *removes the rag.* ROLLY *gags. Coughs. Licks his lips. Starts to cry*]

ROLLY Ah, Jesus.

ELIZABETH Why did you beat Junior up.

ROLLY Ah, Jesus. That was awful. I can't ... breathe ...

ELIZABETH Why did you break in here and beat Junior up. Why?!

[*She holds the rag close to his mouth*]

ROLLY He ripped me off!

ELIZABETH Bullshit.

ROLLY Honest. We had a deal. We made a deal. Then we made a time for a meeting. He was supposed to bring his man to the meeting. His suit man. It was a simple thing. The usual thing. Except when they showed up they were armed. They had serious weapons in their possession. I was not prepared. I don't do crimes with weapons. I'm against it, you know, on principle.

ELIZABETH I told you I don't want to hear this bullshit!

ROLLY They ripped me off! They took my merchandise. That's the simple truth, man. Two big bags full of top-grade stuff. Beautiful stuff. Explicit. You know, *real* explicit.

ELIZABETH [*backs away. Lowers her head*] Ah, shit. [*she goes to the hallway door. Yells upstairs*]

Junior! Junior get down here. Now!

[ELIZABETH *starts to pace. Stops. Looks at* ROLLY. *Shakes her head*] The word is illicit by the way. Not explicit. *Il-lic-it.*

ROLLY Ah, no. I'm sorry. But I think it's explicit.

ELIZABETH Listen, I know the word, asshole. The word to describe your drugs is illicit.

ROLLY Drugs? It wasn't drugs. I don't touch drugs on principle. Also, that's for younger guys. I'm talking porn. You know. *Por-nog-ra-phy.* Real first-rate stuff. You know—explicit.

ELIZABETH What are you talking about.

ROLLY My business is pornography. I'm the king of it. Ask anyone. Been doin' it for years. Some good years, a few bad years. But that's what I do. I sell pictures of naked people doing things to other naked people. And videos. Videos you can't get in any store. The market is huge. And it's growing. I don't know why. There must be a reason for it, you know, a need. I'm just helping people with a need they've got. I don't know, it's a strange—

ELIZABETH Okay. Shut up. Keep your mouth closed.

ROLLY Okay.

[*Long pause*]

ELIZABETH I believe you. I think you're telling the truth, you disgusting little pile of vomit.

ROLLY Thank you.

ELIZABETH Not that it helps me one stinking little bit. Not that I understand how pornography turned into drugs and wound up in—

[**NORA** *comes in*]

Where's Junior.

NORA Gone. I think he went out through a window. And he took the man upstairs with him. What's going on here, Elizabeth. Has this person implicated Junior in some crime. Has he suggested Junior has regressed in some way. That he's a criminal again. What's going on. You can tell me. I know you probably don't want to worry me. You're generous like that. But—

ELIZABETH You're going to have to be quiet for a while, Mom.
I'm thinking.
ROLLY Can I go now.
ELIZABETH No.
ROLLY Can I go later.
ELIZABETH No. Probably not.
ROLLY Well, I have to go sometime. You're not making any
sense. Sooner or later I gotta go. I mean, what else can I do.
I can't just stay. What's the point in that.
ELIZABETH I might need you.
ROLLY Why. I told you all I know. He did that to me. So I did
that to him.
ELIZABETH I might need you! If all this comes together in the
worst possible way. You know, in a meaningless, arbitrary,
pathetic, ugly, destructive way with no true purpose, and
nothing but sad and wretched consequences—well, I might
need an outlet for that! I might need to kill someone. That
might be you! I mean, why the fuck not, eh! Why the fuck
not you! I mean, why the fuck is this happening to my
family. So why the fuck shouldn't you die!!
[*She is shaking* ROLLY]
ROLLY [*to* NORA] Could you help me out here. Maybe calm
her down a bit.
NORA Not when she's like this. Maybe later. Maybe when she's
had a little sleep.
ELIZABETH Good idea. Sleep. Just a little nap. To clear my
head. Wake me in thirty-five minutes. [ELIZABETH *starts
off*]
NORA I will, dear.
ELIZABETH [*stops*] Gag him, Mom. You have to gag him. And
don't let him go. I know in your heart you've already
forgiven him for whatever he's done. But if you let him go,
I'll just have to go get him again.
NORA I know, dear.
ELIZABETH And could you call my office for me, Mom. Tell

them I won't be in for a couple of days.

NORA I'll say you're ill.

ELIZABETH I am ill, Mom. I'm really, really ill. [*She leaves*]

ROLLY You could let me go. I think that'd be okay.

NORA I have to trust Elizabeth on this. Elizabeth is sometimes the only thing this family has going for it in the struggle.

ROLLY What struggle.

NORA *The struggle.* You know. The one out there. [*she is over at the counter looking for something in a drawer*]

ROLLY Oh yeah. The struggle out there is ... really something. [*starts to cry*] That's my struggle, too. The one out there. That's the one where everyone and everything doesn't make sense. And everything you do is wrong. And they find out. And—

NORA You can't talk anymore. Talking doesn't help you anyway. I've noticed that. Talking just makes you wallow and cast blame. I found some tape in the drawer. I'm going to put a piece over your mouth. It's better than the rag. I'm sorry about the rag, I really am. But this tape is better. [*She rips off a piece. Puts it across his mouth. She gets a chair to put next to him*]
I'm going to talk to you now. Talk to you for a long time. Until I get tired and have to go to bed. You have to listen closely and try to understand what I'm saying to you. There's a little trick you can use. When I'm talking don't pretend I'm not really talking about you. Don't let yourself believe I'm saying these things about someone else. Someone neither of us knows. For example. If I say you feel worthless and afraid, you can't say to yourself that's not true. And then not listen when I suggest all the reasons you feel worthless and afraid. Because if you do, you won't understand when I get to the part when I talk about all the ways you can maybe stop feeling worthless and afraid. So that's the trick. Try to understand. And don't pretend.

All right. Get ready. Are you ready.

[ROLLY *nods*]

Good for you.

[*Lights start to fade*]

First. You were born. Right away you shared some experience with everyone else in the world. Everyone in the past, everyone rich and poor, and smart and average. That's a fact. You were born. You were alive in the world. So far so good ...

[*Lights fade.* NORA *is still talking, but we can't hear her*]

[*Blackout*]

Scene Five

ROLLY *alone. Still tied up. Eyes wide*
TOM *and* JUNIOR *come in from the screen door*

TOM Okay. Go make sure they're all asleep.

JUNIOR Are you sure this is a good plan?

TOM Well, it's better than doing nothing.

JUNIOR Are you sure. Maybe doing nothing is better. Maybe it's the best we can do right now ... Okay? So let's do that instead.

TOM Get a hold of yourself. Try to act like a ... you know ...

JUNIOR A what? Try to act like a what?

TOM Forget it. Go check on them.

[JUNIOR *starts off. And passes* ROLLY]

JUNIOR [*to* ROLLY] Look what you did to my arm, asshole.

[*He leaves*]

TOM [*goes to* ROLLY] Okay, listen to this, insect. I'm going to untie you. If you make a move to escape I'll be forced to hurt you. The ugly part of me wants to hurt you anyway, so I won't need much of an excuse to cause you grievous bodily harm. Understand?

[ROLLY *nods*]

Good.

[TOM *starts to untie* ROLLY]

We heard you talking to Elizabeth, insect. We were hiding outside the window here. We heard you deny knowledge of those drugs. Maybe you were telling the truth, maybe you weren't. We will determine that when we get you to a more secluded place. But someone set us up. If it wasn't you, it was your kid. To save your life, insect, you might have to lead us to your kid. Do you think you'll be able to make that decision when the time comes.

[ROLLY *nods*]

That's what I thought.

[JUNIOR *comes back in*]

JUNIOR They're all asleep. How you doin'.

TOM Getting there.

JUNIOR Elizabeth isn't going to like this. She hunted this guy down. She went to a lot of trouble. I mean, look at all the rope she bought.

TOM Yeah. She thinks ahead. She's prepared. She's committed to a job well done. God, I admire her. If she's ever talking to me again I'm going to tell her that.

JUNIOR You know what, man? I don't think that's ever gonna happen. We're finished in this house. This guy told Elizabeth we were doing business with him. That means we're both outta here. They don't really need us anyway. They'll be fine without us. Better.

TOM Get a hold of yourself. You can't talk that way. We have a part to play in this family. We do.

[TOM *has finished untying* ROLLY]

JUNIOR Yeah? What?

TOM We're working that out. That's part of what we're doing. Looking for our purpose … Look, don't fall apart on me here. Think about all of the good things we've done.

JUNIOR Yeah? What were they?

TOM Come on, get a hold of yourself! We've done plenty. We ripped off that gang of break-and-enter artists, and we made them think they'd been ripped off by that other gang of break-and-enter artists. They had a nice little battle about that. Put a few of them out of action. And that guy with the pit bull …

JUNIOR The pimp?

[TOM *pulls* ROLLY *up*]

TOM No! The pimp had the Doberman! The guy with the pit bull had the old Dodge van and that crack house. He doesn't have that crack house anymore.

[*They all start off*]

JUNIOR Oh, right. 'Cause of the pimp with the Doberman.

We took money away from the break-and-enter artists, and
bought some of that pimp's girls away from him and—

TOM Made it look like the guy with the pit bull in the Dodge
van was looking to move into the prostitution business.
And bingo!

JUNIOR The crack house gets burned to the ground! It was
great.

TOM Yeah, it was. Feeling any better?

JUNIOR A little. Someday we gotta get rid of all those
fucking dogs around here. I mean, especially with the
baby around ...
[*They are gone.* NORA *comes in. Goes to the door. Watches a
moment. Turns*]

NORA It's better this way.
[ELIZABETH *comes in. Hair tousled. Blouse outside her skirt.
Barefoot*]

ELIZABETH Mom, I said just thirty-five min— Hey! Where is
he. Where's my prisoner?

NORA Junior and the man you call Dad took him. It's better
this way.

ELIZABETH They had no right! He was mine. I wasn't finished
with him. I just left him down here to stew for a while. [*she
is agitated. Moving around*]

NORA Junior and the man you call Dad know about these
things. They both have past lives with criminal content.
They've probably taken that Rolly person to just the right
place and just the right people in order to resolve this
dilemma. I'm worried about Junior, I'll admit. If something bad happens let's pray it happens to the man you call
Dad.

ELIZABETH Typical bullshit! I do the hard work. Someone else
gets the glory. It's just like at work. This is the same crap
the senior partners are always pulling. It's like there's this
plot to oppress me and wear me down and turn me to
dust. But people still ask me, 'What are you doing for the

environment, minority rights, world peace?' Like I've got time. I work sixty-five hours a week ... I've got a family that's in more or less perpetual crisis, and all I want out of life, I mean really all I want, is just a fucking even break!

NORA Maybe you should get some more sleep, Elizabeth.

ELIZABETH Come on, Mom. I had that little rodent on the edge of collapsing. Telling me things he didn't even know he knew. Junior and Dad aren't the only ones who know about guys like that. I've spent my whole life around guys like that. I'm the fucking expert here! They had no right to interfere.

NORA Are you hungry. Thirsty. Do you want to play a game of cards. [*she quickly takes a deck of cards from a drawer*]

ELIZABETH And what are they up to anyway. Junior and Dad. What are they doing. It can't be anything good. It has to be something stupid and harmful. Rolly said Junior was doing business with him.

NORA [*at the table. Dealing two hands*] You don't believe that, Elizabeth.

ELIZABETH So what are they up to. It's Dad. It's gotta be Dad. Some half-crazy scheme. I detect the particular workings of his brain in this. Some lunatic scheme. We never should have trusted him.

[*Without thinking,* ELIZABETH *sits across from* NORA *and picks up one of the hands*]

NORA I never trusted him, dear. I don't want to say I told you so.

ELIZABETH I thought he was dying! What's going on here. How could he have gone anywhere or taken anyone any-where. He's dying. He's a drooling, mumbling mess!

NORA That was a trick of course, dear. A disguise. I suspected it. This confirms it. If nothing else good comes out of this, we'll all discover the true nature of the man you call Dad.

ELIZABETH [*slams the cards down. Stands*] He is my dad! That's why I call him Dad, Mom. Because he *is!*

[MARY ANN *comes in, wearing a bathrobe and slippers.*
Looking angry]

NORA Hello, Mary Ann. What's wrong. Trouble sleeping?

MARY ANN Gail sent me down. All this shouting is waking up
the baby.

NORA I'm not shouting.

ELIZABETH She means me.

MARY ANN That's right, Elizabeth. I mean you. What's wrong,
Elizabeth. Did you have a hard day. Did someone question
your right to change your mind about something. Perhaps
question your ability to make a choice and stick to it.

ELIZABETH Ah, Jesus Christ.

MARY ANN That's right, Elizabeth. I haven't forgotten. I never
forget. And certain things, I never forgive.

ELIZABETH Go back to bed.

MARY ANN You go back to bed. I don't do things because you
tell me to anymore. I've discovered recently that you can be
very wrong about things. Dad, for example. You were
wrong about him. He's nice. I like him. There. What are
you going to do about that.

ELIZABETH Didn't I tell you before if you didn't stop acting
and talking like an idiot I was going to do something about
it.

MARY ANN I remember words to that effect. But so what. I'm
not afraid of you anymore. And do you know why. You're
inconsistent. Seriously inconsistent. Mom, I have something to tell you. Elizabeth is not a lesbian. Elizabeth will
sleep with anyone. She hasn't made any hard decisions at
all.

[ELIZABETH *has her teeth clenched. She is approaching*
MARY ANN]

ELIZABETH Please go back to bed.

MARY ANN No.

ELIZABETH I don't want to hurt you.

MARY ANN I don't care if you want to hurt me or not. I'm on a

83

voyage of self-discovery. I can't be stopped. You're part of that voyage. Getting to the truth about you. There are other things on this voyage, of course, but I'm dealing with you right now. Who knows. Tomorrow I might deal with Mom. Dealing with things is all I care about.

ELIZABETH Really. You don't care about the police, and the drug charges, or any of that.

MARY ANN Those aren't my problems. I can only deal with myself. And things that affect myself. My personal self. My unconscious self. Clare taught me that.

ELIZABETH Then Clare should be killed. I'll do it. Give me her address. Give it to me! Now!

[ELIZABETH *makes a wild grab for* MARY ANN. MARY ANN *backs away*]

NORA Who is Clare.

ELIZABETH The devil!

MARY ANN My therapist!

NORA You don't need a therapist, Mary Ann. You just need a good friend. That's why you're so sensitive about Elizabeth. You never developed a friendship with anyone else. You rely on your sister too much.

MARY ANN Thanks, Mom. I know that. Clare told me. Clare also told me you almost crippled me emotionally for life, Mom.

ELIZABETH Clare is a dead woman. She's going to die a terrible, brutal death.

[ELIZABETH *is stalking* MARY ANN *around the kitchen table*]

MARY ANN Sure. I understand. I knew you'd feel that way at first. I also know you think I'm selfish. But so what!

[ELIZABETH *grabs* MARY ANN. *Puts her over her shoulder*]

Okay, okay. Clare also taught me the value of the apology.

[ELIZABETH *puts* MARY ANN *inside the broom closet. Closes the door*]

[*from inside the closet*] I know I've hurt people and disappointed people myself. The two of you, for example. So, as well as taking care of myself in an inner way, I'm taking care of others in an outer way. That's why I cook for you. That's why I fixed the strap on your briefcase, Elizabeth. Before I went to sleep I fixed it and put it back beside your bed. You don't have to thank me. I didn't do it for thanks! I did it for mythic reasons! Symbolic reasons! The reasons of dreams!

ELIZABETH You're nuts! You're out of your goddamn mind!

MARY ANN [comes out of the closet holding a box of Bisquick and a muffin pan] Says who?!

ELIZABETH Me! Me! And her. [points to NORA] She'd say it too, if she wasn't so nice, and she wasn't your mother. Everyone would say it. Everyone on the planet who had to listen to you for more than five seconds!!

[GAIL comes rushing in]

GAIL Hey, hey come on! The baby! Your voice is bouncing off the walls.

MARY ANN Sorry.

ELIZABETH She means me!!

GAIL Yeah. What's wrong with you, anyway.

ELIZABETH What makes you think something is wrong with me. I mean, you were on my back before for not getting involved in this family's problems like I should. So now I'm involved. And ... this ... is ... what ... I'm ... like ... when I'm involved!!

GAIL Keep your voice down!!

MARY ANN Yeah. There's no reason to shout. I express very personal, upsetting feelings without shouting. You can do the same.

ELIZABETH [throws her arms up in the air] I need a drink. [she starts searching through the cupboards]

GAIL Hey. Where's that guy who was tied up here before.

MARY ANN Oh, yeah. I didn't notice.

ELIZABETH [mocking] 'Oh yeah. I didn't notice.' I'm a good person, but I didn't notice. I cook for people, do things for people, tell people what their problems are, but I don't notice anything … My name is Mary Ann, and I'm looking for a job. Do you have anything a semi-conscious idiot with a lot of opinions could do … Where's that bottle of scotch. It used to be under the sink.

GAIL [*to* NORA] So where is he. The guy.

NORA Junior took him.

GAIL To the police?

ELIZABETH We don't think so. That would not be our first guess.

GAIL Yeah. So where did he take him.

ELIZABETH Our first guess would be some unpopulated and heavily wooded area just outside the city. Somewhere the ground isn't too hard for digging. Where's my scotch. Who took my scotch. I left it under the sink. It's not there.

MARY ANN Are you that messed up, Elizabeth. You leave bottles in places. Do you leave them everywhere you visit.

ELIZABETH No. Just anywhere you might be.

NORA I didn't know it was yours. I took it, Elizabeth. I threw it out. I thought it belonged to someone else. You know … [*points upstairs*]

MARY ANN The baby?

NORA The man.

GAIL What's she talking about, Mom.

NORA Who, dear.

GAIL Elizabeth. She's saying Junior took that guy out to the country to kill him. Is that right.

NORA Is that what you were saying, Elizabeth.

ELIZABETH [*looking in other cupboards now*] It was just a guess. You wouldn't have any other alcohol in the house would you, Mom. Of course not. Not since Dad got drunk that last time and tried to kill us all. That was a stupid question. I'm sorry for asking, Mom. How about rubbing alcohol, lighter fluid, glue?

[GAIL *goes to* ELIZABETH. *Starts to follow her around*]

86

GAIL So, why would Junior want to kill that guy.

ELIZABETH He's one of the guys who beat him up.

GAIL Yeah. I know that. But that wouldn't be enough of a reason. What are you getting at.

ELIZABETH Relax. It was just a guess. I could be wrong. I'm wrong sometimes. Right, Mary Ann? Hey Mom, where's that stuff you spray on frying pans. I hear you can get a buzz off that.

MARY ANN Stop her, Mom. She's doing that thing she does. When she's overloading. I don't like it.

NORA Elizabeth, you're scaring your sisters.

GAIL Elizabeth. I want you to stop for a moment.

ELIZABETH In a moment. In a moment I'll stop for a moment. Right now I need something. A little something.

MARY ANN You better stop her, Gail.

ELIZABETH [*mocking*] 'You better stop her, Gail.' [*searching frantically now. Pulling things out of the cupboards*] Stop her before she says something, does something, finds something. She's doing that thing she does, Mom. What thing, dear. The thing she does when she's falling apart, Mom. Had it up to here, Mom. Right up to the fucking nose. Right here. Almost full. Filled right up. Just can't take much more …

[GAIL *grabs her.* ELIZABETH *shakes her off*]

Get off! Get the fuck off! I'm on a mission here. A mission of self-fulfilment. This one's for me, Mom. I'm enjoying this. I'm going to rip this home apart, Mom. I think it's time you moved, anyway. Moved everyone, the whole family. My family. The one I'm responsible for!

[GAIL *grabs her.* MARY ANN *is moving closer to them*]

GAIL [*to* MARY ANN] Help me!

ELIZABETH Let me go! You have to let me go. I gotta go. Let me go you little bitch before I rip your scalp off!

GAIL [*to* MARY ANN] Help me!

MARY ANN Okay.

[MARY ANN *grabs* ELIZABETH. *They are both trying to put her on the floor*]

ELIZABETH Ah, shit. This won't work. This will only make me mad. Jesus. Get away from me. Get off me. You're trying to kill me. Aren't you. You want to kill me. I know you do. Ah, here's some hair. What happens if I just pull a little.
[MARY ANN *screams*]
I like that sound. I like that sound a lot.
[MARY ANN *screams*]

MARY ANN Let go!

ELIZABETH You let go!

GAIL Don't! Don't let go. We've almost got her down.
[ELIZABETH *grabs* GAIL*'s hair. Now she has them both by the hair*]

ELIZABETH You've got miles to go before I'm down, kid. I'm absolutely indestructible. Right, Mom. I'm a rock. Aren't I, Mom. A rock. A rock doesn't go down.

GAIL Trip her!

MARY ANN How?!

GAIL Just trip her. Put your foot out!

ELIZABETH How about another little pull on the hair, sis!
[MARY ANN *screams*. GAIL *screams*]

MARY ANN I hate you! Stop that!

GAIL Ouch! Shit! Trip her!

MARY ANN I'm trying!
[*The three of them are swaying back and forth.* ELIZABETH *in the middle. A tangle of arms and hands*]

ELIZABETH They're weak, Mom! Very weak. Gail talks tough, but she's really a pussycat. And Mary Ann's, well … Mary Ann's a shadow. My shadow. And my pussycat. Look at them. Mom. I'm still up. I'm still standing. If you need a daughter to rely on, Mom, I'm the one. Call me anytime. Call me night or day. [*sings*] *Call me. Don't be afraid to just call me.* But you do, don't you. You all call me. You all call me, and call me, and call me … !!

[*Finally* MARY ANN *succeeds in putting a foot behind* ELIZABETH. GAIL *pushes.* ELIZABETH *falls. They fall on top of her*]

GAIL Okay! We've got her. Don't let go.

MARY ANN Don't you let go!

GAIL Okay, Mom. Do it!

MARY ANN Hurry, Mom. We can't hold her much longer. Come on!

[NORA *is nodding. She gets down on her knees beside them*]

GAIL Quick, Mom!

[NORA *opens up the bottom two buttons of* ELIZABETH'*s blouse. Leans over. And starts to blow on* ELIZABETH'*s stomach, giving her a huge raspberry.* ELIZABETH'*s groaning and yelling gradually subside and slowly turn into laughter. The laughter grows.* MARY ANN *and* GAIL *sit back on the floor.* NORA *continues to blow on* ELIZABETH'*s stomach.* ELIZABETH *is laughing hysterically*]

It still works.

MARY ANN Thank God.

NORA [*stands*] I remember the first time I tried that. She'd been sent home from school for punching two little boys. The little boys had punched her first but the teacher wouldn't believe her. Elizabeth was in a rage. I was desperate. Are you all right now, dear.

ELIZABETH I'm fine, Mom. [*giggles*] I love that. Do that again.

NORA Maybe later … I'm going to put the kettle on.

MARY ANN [*getting up*] I'll make toast.

[*Pause.* ELIZABETH *is sighing happily*]

GAIL Elizabeth.

ELIZABETH What, honey.

GAIL I'm really worried about Junior.

ELIZABETH Oh. [*she sits up. Hugs* GAIL] He's all right. He's fine. I was just being pissy. They probably took that guy and handed him over to the cops.

GAIL Really? You really think so.

89

ELIZABETH Yeah. I really do. [*hugs her tight*] I love you.

GAIL I love you, too. I'm sorry you're such a frigging mess.

ELIZABETH So am I.

GAIL Maybe you should stop practising law. Stop doing all that political stuff you do. Take a vacation or something.

ELIZABETH No. No, I— Okay. Yeah. Maybe you could come with me. Take a little break from young motherhood.

GAIL Can't afford it.

ELIZABETH I'll pay. We'll go away together. Some place soft and warm.

MARY ANN Can I come too.

ELIZABETH & GAIL No.

MARY ANN I know you don't mean that.

GAIL Yes—

ELIZABETH We do.

MARY ANN No you don't. I know you don't. I'm coming. Wherever you go. I'm coming. You love each other. But you love me, too. I know that. I'm confident about that. They love me, don't they Mom.

NORA Of course they love you. They were taught to love you. I paid special attention to that part of their education. I knew there would be times it would be easier not to love you. Because of your … well, because of your—

MARY ANN Gee, Mom. I was only kidding. When I asked you if they loved me it was just a joke. I feel like crying.

NORA Why?

MARY ANN Well, because of what you just said. That's sad. That you had to teach them to love me. That's so very sad.

ELIZABETH [*getting up*] She's going to tell Clare about that, Mom. Clare is going to have a lot to say about what that means. [*to* GAIL] Clare is Mary Ann's therapist.

GAIL [*smiles*] I thought she was her hairdresser.

MARY ANN Clare loves me.

[ELIZABETH *goes over. Puts her arms around* MARY ANN]

ELIZABETH No, Mary Ann. We love you. Clare just thinks

you're very interesting.

MARY ANN What do you want on your toast.

ELIZABETH Cocoa.

MARY ANN No way. I hate that. That's disgusting.

[ELIZABETH *grabs* MARY ANN *by the hair*]

ELIZABETH It's my toast, Mary Ann. You asked me. I told you. Put cocoa on my toast. Lots of cocoa. Okay?

MARY ANN Sure … Gail? … Jam? Marmalade?

GAIL I've got to go back to bed.

MARY ANN You can't. We're all here. We're together. The four of us. We're never together anymore just the four of us.

GAIL So what.

MARY ANN It's the family. It's us. Just us.

GAIL The family has grown a bit since you last looked in on it, Mary Ann. I've got to get up with the baby. [*she starts off*] Goodnight. [*stops. Looks at* ELIZABETH] Is there something you're not telling me about Junior.

ELIZABETH No. Junior's fine. Don't worry about him.

GAIL Because he's my life, you know. A large part of it. If he's going down the drain, so am I.

ELIZABETH I wouldn't let that happen.

GAIL You wouldn't?

ELIZABETH Trust me. Go upstairs. Get your daughter. Get in bed. Hug her. Go to sleep.

[ELIZABETH *hugs* GAIL]

GAIL See you in the morning.

[*She leaves*]

NORA [*to* MARY ANN] You're sad, aren't you. Feeling guilty about leaving your daughter. Gail is going up to sleep with her daughter, and this makes you feel empty, hollow, hard … Doesn't it, Mary Ann.

MARY ANN Yeah, Mom. A bit. I guess. So?

NORA So what, dear.

MARY ANN So, what should I do.

NORA I wouldn't give you advice about that, dear. What could

I possibly say. You're the expert about your own life. I have a great deal of respect for experts of any kind. Besides, you have so many things on your mind. Things I could barely understand even if I had the desire to listen to them. Things more important than your only child, the child you brought into this world. Things you've recently found out at ... at that place where you said you are ... Where was that place again, dear.

MARY ANN Crossroads. I'm at a crossroads. Your toast is in the ... thing. I'm going to bed. [*she starts off. Stops*] I am, though. I really am at a crossroads ... Whatever the hell that means. Dammit.

[*She leaves*]

ELIZABETH She'll go home to her daughter, Mom. She always does.

NORA But why does she leave in the first place. That's what we have to find out. The constant leaving of her only child is mysterious. And distressing. What is it that makes her do it.

ELIZABETH Her father deserted *her*. Maybe she's just repeating a pattern.

NORA Why? Why is she repeating a pattern ... When her father left that last time she was ... how old?

ELIZABETH Fifteen? Sixteen? Something like that.

NORA Are those difficult years in a person's life.

ELIZABETH All the years in Mary Ann's life have been difficult, Mom. All the months, weeks, days, hours, and minutes. And the older she gets the worse she gets ... You have to stop worrying about her, Mom. She just basically has a difficult time living. The only solution would be to put her out of her misery ... Harden your heart, put her in a sack and drown her like a kitten ... That was just a joke, Mom.

NORA I know, dear ... And I know Mary Ann could never actually be happy. She'll never be ... light-hearted. But I suspect she has deeper problems than we're giving her credit for. Something unresolved about her father.

ELIZABETH Look Mom, we've all got something unresolved about Dad. Something deep and horrible. I don't think Mary Ann's in any worse shape about him than the rest of us.

NORA She deserts her child! There's nothing worse a mother can do. Don't be stupid!

[*Pause*]

I'm sorry.

ELIZABETH That's okay. Why don't you yell at her like that, Mom. It might help.

NORA Yelling doesn't help Mary Ann. You've been yelling at Mary Ann for years ... I have to tell you something, Elizabeth. It's about that man you call your father ... Guess what. I know he really is your father. I know that. I'm not insane about that. That's good news isn't it, Elizabeth. So far so good. And I actually had a very good reason for not acknowledging him. For the first time in years I had something he needed. Needed badly ... Do you want to know what it was. Recognition! The power of simple recognition ... Of course, I just stumbled across this power. I came to it accidentally. But once I had it I used it without remorse. You see, when he first came back after what ... ten years?

ELIZABETH I think so.

NORA Yes. Ten. Anyway, when he came back I had a severe shock, a terrible thing happened. I saw him. And right away I wanted to kill myself. I thought I'd rather be dead than go through any more awful experiences with him. Of course, I couldn't do that because of you and your sisters. I couldn't leave you alone with him. So I came up with another way. I just pretended he was someone else. I don't know where I got the idea, but it seemed to work all right. It meant it wasn't necessary for me to have anything to do with him. And you girls could have a father if you needed one.

ELIZABETH Why are you telling me this, Mom. Because of Mary Ann?

NORA Circumstances change. The needs of people change. What this family needs now is something more clear. Clearer roles. Lighter burdens for ... some of us. [*she starts off. Stops*] You know, Elizabeth, I have a theory about why bad things keep happening to this family. Do you want to hear it.

ELIZABETH [*sighs*] Sure, Mom.

NORA I think we believe that we don't deserve to be happy. I know Mary Ann believes it's just fate. But Mary Ann is too distressed to think clearly about these things. My theory is better. We're running away from happiness. We think we need to struggle, and suffer, and work really hard before we can just stay still, and let happiness catch up and surround us. What do you think about that theory, Elizabeth.

ELIZABETH It scares me, Mom.

NORA Oh. Then just forget about it. I could be wrong ... Do you think Mary Ann's theory is better.

ELIZABETH Not really.

[NORA *gestures, shrugs. She wants to say something soothing.* ELIZABETH *turns away*]

NORA Goodnight, Elizabeth.

ELIZABETH Goodnight, Mom.

[NORA *hesitates. Then leaves.* ELIZABETH *wraps her arms around herself. Shudders. Looks around. Begins to clean up some of the mess she made earlier*]

[*Blackout*]

[*Intermission*]

Scene Six

Later

ELIZABETH *is at the table. Head down*

TOM, JUNIOR *and* ROLLY *come in.* TOM *has* ROLLY *by the scruff of the neck. They are all dirty and wet*

ROLLY Please, please let me go. I did what you asked. I tried to help you find my kid Stevie. I took you to all our special places. Why won't you let me go.

JUNIOR [*whispering*] Shut up. [*to* TOM] Who is that at the table. Oh no. Is that Elizabeth.

TOM [*whispering*] Yeah.

JUNIOR Shit.

TOM It's okay. She's asleep. If we're quiet we won't—

ROLLY She's waiting! She's been waiting for me! She can't wait to get her hands on me. Let me go!

JUNIOR Shush!

[TOM *whacks* ROLLY *on the head*]

ROLLY Geez! That hurt!

JUNIOR Shut up. Shut your mouth!

ROLLY He hurt me. Geez! He hit me with his knuckles. I'm dizzy.

TOM [*calmly*] Look. I'm trying not to really hurt you. I'm trying to control a really ugly, violent urge I've got to take away your face.

ROLLY Take away my face? What's that mean.

JUNIOR What should we do.

TOM Tie him up again.

JUNIOR What good will that do.

TOM At least things will be the way we found them. We didn't accomplish anything by taking him so the least we can do is put him back where he was.

[*They start to tie him up*]

ROLLY Oh no, don't do this. There's no purpose in this. Look, the truth is the women in this house are kinda spooky. The mother—she's a nice lady, I guess, but she just wants to talk to me all the time. She talked to me for hours. She said things that really bothered me. Really personal things about me. Like she knows me or something. Knows all about my life. It's spooky. And this one here. The one you call Elizabeth. She's something else. She's like a monster of some kind. She comes across as some kind of evil thing from some other planet. No offence. I know you're related. But she's worse than guys I've met in prison who kill people with saws. You can't give me back to her! You keep me!

TOM She hunted you down. You belong to her.

JUNIOR We just borrowed you.

ROLLY [*crying*] I can't stay. It's spooky here! While I was sitting here before, these two other women came in, with a baby in a stroller. Just came in, saw me all tied up. And they just smiled at each other and went upstairs. Like having a frigging prisoner in the kitchen, some guy tied up like a frigging dead pig, was a normal thing. I can't stay here. I can't, I can't, I can't!

[TOM *whacks* ROLLY *hard.* ROLLY *is unconscious. They continue to tie him up*]

JUNIOR Did you have to do that.

TOM Yeah. That's the least I had to do. I've told you, I've still got these ugly things inside me. Things that get stirred up by stuff like this. By scum like this. I'm trying hard to change, but sometimes—

JUNIOR Can we talk about this later. Let's just get out of here before Elizabeth wakes up.

TOM She must be a tired person to sleep through all of that. Do you think she works too hard. I've heard them talking about her. Nora and Gail. They say she's working herself to death.

JUNIOR Look. We have to talk about this later. I'm depressed. This whole thing is really depressing.

TOM And confusing. Why aren't things working out better for us. We have good motives. We admit our shortcomings. Why wasn't his kid at any of those places.

JUNIOR And why were those places so disgusting. Do you think they really live in that sewer. Who can live in a sewer, man. Or that bush by the railway tracks. I mean a bush, man. They had a little clearing inside a bush. Talk about depressing.

TOM Get a hold of yourself.

JUNIOR Stop telling me to get a hold of myself. That doesn't help. Try to say something that helps. Anything.

TOM Okay. He's all tied up. Just the way he was. Let's get out of here.

JUNIOR Okay.

[*Their backs are to* ELIZABETH. *She sits up suddenly. Eyes wild*]

ELIZABETH Stay exactly where you are!

[JUNIOR *and* TOM *jump.* ELIZABETH *stands. Walks around them. Looking at them. Hard*]

JUNIOR [*to* TOM] We should explain to her. She looks like she definitely wants an explanation.

ELIZABETH Be quiet, Junior. I don't want you to talk right now. I want this man here to talk. This man here who's not supposed to be able to talk. This man here who is supposed to be sick. Dying.

JUNIOR [*to* TOM] She wants to hear it from you. [*to* ELIZABETH] Can I go upstairs, then. Gail is probably worried.

ELIZABETH Stay where you are. Gail's asleep. And when this man here tells his story I might need you to verify it ... [*to* TOM] Go ahead.

TOM I ... don't know where to start. How much did you hear. I mean, when did you wake up.

ELIZABETH I wasn't asleep.

JUNIOR [*whimpers*] I'm feeling a little sick to my stomach.

TOM Cut that out. Act like a you-know.

ELIZABETH A what?

TOM Let Junior go upstairs, Elizabeth. You and I can work this out. Junior is nervous. Aren't you.

JUNIOR Yeah.

TOM And he's making me nervous. He's so scared of you. He's making me scared of you. And that's not natural. I'm your father. We can work this out.

ELIZABETH He stays. If anyone is leaving it's you. And I don't mean upstairs to your cozy room. I mean out that door. Now what in God's name are you up to! Speak!

TOM Okay. So first, you're probably wondering why I seem better all of a sudden.

ELIZABETH No. I've figured that out. Skip to the part where you explain everything bad that's happened to this family lately, and how you're responsible.

JUNIOR She's smart. Sometimes I can't believe how smart she is. You'd better tell her.

TOM I'm going to tell her!

JUNIOR You better tell her fast! See that look in her eyes. I've seen that look before. Tell her before she does something!

TOM Okay! Okay, yeah … [to ELIZABETH] I had a plan.

JUNIOR I just want to make that part clear. *He* had a plan. Okay?

TOM It was a plan I got all of a sudden. It came from a bad place in me, I think. It was a good plan, but it came from a bad place. From guilt. I got this idea, this plan, because I felt so bad for what I'd put you through. All the bad—

ELIZABETH Yeah, I got it. What was the plan.

TOM At first it wasn't a plan. It was just a feeling. I heard about what was going on in this part of the city. I read about it in the newspapers. I saw how things were deteriorating. The crime, the awful victimization—

ELIZABETH Okay. Be quiet. That's enough.

TOM No, but I haven't—!

ELIZABETH I said that's enough! I got it. I know what you did.

JUNIOR She's amazing. You didn't tell her, really. But she knows. She's unbelievable.

ELIZABETH No. I just know him. Know how his mind works. He went into his protector mode. He hatched some plan to clean up the neighbourhood.

JUNIOR Amazing.

ELIZABETH And he sucked you right into the middle of it.

JUNIOR Right. Right into the middle. I got sucked in.

ELIZABETH You idiot!

JUNIOR Right again!

TOM We infiltrated. From this feeling I had we developed a complex and daring plan to make contact with all the criminal elements in this neighbourhood. And then by trickery and theft make them think they were being double-crossed by each other.

JUNIOR And that would start a war.

TOM A crime war. A war in which they would all be destroyed or made totally ineffective. Like I said, it was a complex plan.

JUNIOR I never really understood it.

TOM It was beyond understanding. It was designed to operate on momentum. It was a plan that came from deep inside me. A mixture of things from my experience and my heart.

JUNIOR A plan of love, really.

TOM And anger and regret.

JUNIOR And fear. At least for me. Fear was a big part of the plan.

ELIZABETH But that old standby 'stupid' was the biggest part, right?

TOM We each had a part to play. I was the money man. The suit man.

JUNIOR I worked the streets.

TOM He did pretty good. I'm proud of him in many ways. [to JUNIOR] I haven't told you that till now.

99

JUNIOR Thanks.

ELIZABETH But something went wrong! Something always goes wrong ... What was it!

JUNIOR We don't know.

TOM We think we were set up. I know we can find out who did it. But it will take time.

ELIZABETH You've got six hours. Is that time enough.

JUNIOR I don't think so. It usually takes us a few hours just to talk about what we're going to do, and then the first thing we do is usually wrong, so we have to—

TOM Why six hours.

ELIZABETH You see, I've been carrying around this little secret. Dying to share it with someone because it was driving me crazy, making me so scared it was killing me. I might as well share it with you two. Why not. You're here. You both seem to be part of my life for some predetermined sickening reason.

TOM Elizabeth! You're talking like your mother, God bless her. But this is not the time. Talk the way I taught you when you were a kid.

ELIZABETH He means like him. He taught me to talk like him. He let Mary Ann talk like Mom, God bless her. But that was quite enough of that. I needed to talk in a way that got things done.

TOM Elizabeth. Why do we only have six hours.

ELIZABETH [*stares at* TOM. *Speaks very clearly*] When I went to get Mom away from those cops I cut a deal. They gave me until eight o'clock this morning to come up with the person or persons who put those drugs in our basement. Failing that they are going to arrest my mother, God bless her, and charge her with possession for the purpose of trafficking.

JUNIOR Really?

ELIZABETH Really.

JUNIOR [*to* TOM] We can't let that happen.

ELIZABETH [*turns to* JUNIOR] Don't look at him when you say that. He can't help you. He's a total fuck up. [*to* TOM] Aren't you. Aren't you?!

TOM I ... just wanted—

ELIZABETH What, what did you want?! To take care of us again?! To be in charge again?! To have us in your debt again?! What! ... What!

TOM To help! Maybe I wasn't thinking clearly. Okay, I wasn't. But I was isolated. Wasn't allowed to be in the family. Had to pretend to be sick ... All that made me not think straight.

ELIZABETH Sad ... Jesus. [*to* JUNIOR] That's his excuse. He wasn't allowed in the family so his mind got cloudy. What's yours.

JUNIOR I don't know. I didn't know he had a cloudy mind. What he said sounded right to me. All the crime around here. Maybe it was the baby. Maybe having the baby made me extra worried. Maybe it made me cloudy, too.

ELIZABETH [*to* TOM] You're a plague. And a curse. You're a life-long, enormous, black hole of misery to this family.

TOM I'm trying to change. I just ... Well, you see, I ... [*mumbles something*]

ELIZABETH What. What did you say.

[TOM *goes to* JUNIOR. *Whispers in his ear*]

JUNIOR He loves you.

ELIZABETH What!

[TOM *whispers in* JUNIOR*'s ear*]

JUNIOR He loves this family.

ELIZABETH He loves us. He loves us?! Amazing! Can you imagine what he'd do to this family if he hated us. The mind boggles. I don't know, could be anything ... little nuclear devices shoved up all our assholes!

[*A knock at the back door.* DIAN *is standing there*]

DIAN Hi. Can I come in.

[*They all look at each other.* JUNIOR *starts to cry*]

We got a call about a prowler around your house ... Can I

come in.

[ELIZABETH *goes to* ROLLY. *Sits on his lap. Puts an arm around his neck*]

ELIZABETH Sure.

[DIAN *comes in*]

DIAN Thanks. One of your neighbours saw someone suspicious looking. I took the call. I thought it might give me a chance to see how you were getting along with our little problem. Any solutions to that yet?

ELIZABETH What about the prowler.

DIAN I looked around. Seems fine. Probably just some kid. So ... you didn't answer my question.

ELIZABETH We have till eight o'clock. That was the deal.

DIAN Pretty stupid deal if you ask me. That was my ex-partner's idea ... Deadlines ... That was the last stupid idea I could take hearing from him. I asked to work alone. I mean, the guy's a throwback. You probably recognized his type right away, Elizabeth. He's the kind of cop you must see a lot of in your work.

ELIZABETH Yeah. What are you doing here. Really.

DIAN I told you. Really. You seem hostile, Elizabeth. I don't blame you. But you've got to believe me when I say I just want to help you. You'll notice I haven't asked you about your hostage here. That's because I don't want to cramp your style.

[ELIZABETH *gets off* ROLLY*'s lap. Goes to* JUNIOR. *Gives him a quick whack.* JUNIOR *stops crying*]

People need plenty of space to wheel and deal in things like this. This could be a matter entirely within the family. A family might need years to iron out something like this. Get someone to admit a wrongdoing. There's so much going on in most families. More in this one, I'll bet. The human interaction in this family is extremely complex. That would be my guess. But you still didn't answer my question. Are you any closer to finding out who put all that illegal substance in your basement.

ELIZABETH We're working on it.

DIAN Hi, Junior. How's the arm.

JUNIOR All right.

DIAN [to TOM] You must be the father. We haven't met. [she puts out her hand] I'm Dian Black, O.C.S.

TOM Hi.

[They shake]

DIAN You guys look kind of messed up. And you don't smell so good, either. Been down in the sewers, have you. Searching for a rat? No, no don't answer that. I was just thinking out loud.

ELIZABETH Why don't you just go away. I told you I was working on it.

DIAN Well, I'm glad you're working on it, Elizabeth. But working on it might not be enough unless there's a methodology involved. There could be forces at play here beyond your knowledge. I'm about to stick my neck out here, Elizabeth. You have to appreciate that, appreciate all the implications of that vis-à-vis my career, my personal safety.

TOM What's wrong with you. You talk like you're on drugs.

JUNIOR Yeah.

DIAN Shush. I'm talking to the brains in the family now. Right, Elizabeth? Now like I said, I don't want to cramp your style, but your hostage here is a dead end. He's just a victim of Junior's shenanigans. That's right! We know about the avenging angels here. We know. And we don't care. Not the people I work for anyway ... But hey, wait a minute ... my ex-partner, he might feel different. [to TOM] You know him, don't you Tom. You know Mike Dixon. [she takes out her lip balm. Applies it casually]

TOM We worked together for a while. A long time ago.

DIAN The Mike Dixons of this world have long-term memories. You see, this is leading somewhere, Elizabeth. Ever do anything to him that might deserve a payback, Tom. No, don't answer that! Just think about it. I mean, that was just an example, anyway. You get my drift, Elizabeth. You see how I'm opening up the possibilities here. I mean if a cop, a certain kind of cop, or a number of cops, are very, very annoyed with someone, well ... they always think in terms of ... well, revenge may be too strong a word, but—

ELIZABETH It's me, isn't it. This was a set-up to pressure me. To neutralize me.

DIAN How did you do that. Get into the middle of my thought process like that. No one has ever done that. Wow. Okay. We have to be careful now. Vis-à-vis our personal safety, our careers. Maybe we should talk about this alone, in another room.

ELIZABETH [*lost in thought*] What?

DIAN I was trying to open up your mind to the possibilities. If we're going to actually discuss this, Elizabeth, we have to be alone.

ELIZABETH I should have seen it. What other possible reason could anyone have to frame this family ... I thought it was you, Junior. I thought it was because of your past somehow. [*to* TOM] Then I thought it was you. Some hairy bullshit you were involved in beyond human understanding.

TOM Well, actually it could be me.

JUNIOR He was involved in hairy bullshit beyond human understanding.

ELIZABETH No. It's me. Shit!

DIAN I can help you with this, Elizabeth. But we have to be discreet.

ELIZABETH I'm not sure I want your help, Dian. So go fuck yourself. I think I owe my family an explanation.

TOM You don't owe me anything, honey. Let's just call it even.

ELIZABETH Get serious. [*to* JUNIOR] Did you hear what he just said.

JUNIOR He didn't really mean that, Elizabeth ...

[*to* TOM] How the hell can you be even, man. Did she try to burn the house down and shit like that.

TOM It was just an expression!

ELIZABETH Unbelievable.

JUNIOR I wouldn't mind an explanation, Elizabeth. Just hearing something that makes sense would—

ELIZABETH I was just getting really sick and tired of defending people who'd had their brains beaten out in the back seats of cruisers, in the basements of police stations. I've made some enemies on the force. I've been writing them, calling them, threatening to go to the press. Well, I couldn't help myself. I was just plain sick of it. No big deal. I'm sick of so much I see. Sure, most of the little pricks I defend are guilty as hell, but I don't see that gives the state any right to knock out their teeth. [*to* TOM] So I complained. And I tried to organize other people, lawyers mostly, so they could complain.

DIAN Bad timing, Elizabeth. You caught the police force at a particularly sensitive moment, is what I think. They've received so much negative press. Personally, I'm on your side, but professionally I gotta say I think I know where they're coming from.

ELIZABETH This is criminal conspiracy we're talking about, Dian. That's a very large risk to take just to shut me up. It sounds like the product of an unstable mind ...

DIAN Maybe ... Maybe. But is there a possible deal here, Elizabeth. Name-calling aside. Can you offer something here. Do you have a message you want me to take down-town vis-à-vis your public campaign against police brutal-ity. Or do we let your mom go to jail. Come on, Elizabeth. You know how it works! Make an offer for chrissake!

[*Pause*]

ELIZABETH I'm willing to talk about it.

DIAN A settlement which will satisfy all parties.

ELIZABETH We'll talk about it.

DIAN Without prejudice?

ELIZABETH That'll be talked about.

DIAN Can I use the phone.

ELIZABETH Sure. Go ahead.

DIAN This has to be a private call, Elizabeth. Is there another one somewhere.

ELIZABETH In the hall upstairs.

DIAN Thank you. This shouldn't take long.

[*She hurries off*]

JUNIOR Who is she calling.

TOM I'd say her boss. Someone higher up.

JUNIOR [*to* ELIZABETH] Do you really think she's trying to help us.

ELIZABETH I don't know. She's hard to read.

TOM She doesn't talk like a cop. At first I thought she talked like a drug addict. I was close. She talks like a politician. Maybe she's up to something, you know ... political. Or maybe it's a woman thing.

ELIZABETH Jesus. What's that supposed to mean.

TOM Some woman sees some other woman in a tight spot. So she, you know, feels something about that only a woman could feel.

ELIZABETH You mean something human? Like sympathy? Look, don't answer that. I don't want to talk to you anymore. I didn't mean to talk to you in the first place. I forgot.

TOM I'm glad you forgot. I enjoyed talking to you. Whatever happens, I'll always remember these last couple of minutes.

JUNIOR He means that, Elizabeth.

ELIZABETH Be quiet. Both of you ... Why are you defending him, Junior. Have the two of you 'bonded' or something. Has this sad and meaningless experience helped you form some pathetic, mutually destructive relationship. Don't you think this family has enough of those already.

[STEVIE *suddenly appears at the basement door. Holding a gun*]

STEVIE Okay. Hands up. Up high. Really high. Come on!

ELIZABETH How did you get into our basement again. We had that window fixed. We put bars on that window.

STEVIE So what. You think bars mean anything to me? I do this for a living for chrissake.

[TOM *takes a step towards* STEVIE]

TOM Do you want me to take that weapon away from this insect, Elizabeth.

ELIZABETH Stay out of this. [*to* STEVIE] What do you want.

STEVIE Whatya mean what do I want. I want my dad. You can't just take a guy's dad away like that. Look at him. He's been tortured or something. You rotten bastards … Untie him … Come on, untie him!

ELIZABETH [*to* JUNIOR] Do it.

[JUNIOR *starts to untie* ROLLY]

STEVIE Hey, not the guy with the broken arm, man. That'll take hours. You think I'm stupid? I want someone with two arms to untie him. You rotten bastards. Look at him. I hate the way he looks. Wake him up. Slap him or something.

TOM My pleasure.

STEVIE Hey, I heard that, you pig. Okay, I changed my mind. Splash him with water. Come on. You. The woman. Get water. Splash him. You. The guy with two arms. Untie him. Well, what are you waiting for. Do it. Do it, you pigs!

[TOM *is approaching* STEVIE. STEVIE *is backing away*]

TOM Okay. Look, I'm going to do what you ask. But I'm warning you, for your own safety, to be careful how you talk to us.

STEVIE Jesus! He's threatening me. I've got a gun. But he doesn't care. He wants to hurt someone so bad he doesn't care about guns or anything. What's wrong with you people. You're all crazy-mean. Jesus!!

ELIZABETH [*moving to get a pot, which is sitting on the stove beside a burner. To* STEVIE] You're getting yourself all worked up here. Why don't you just put that gun away. We'll give you back your dad. And the two of you can just … leave.

[*She throws a pot of liquid on* ROLLY. *He starts to stir.* ELIZABETH *begins to untie him*]

STEVIE Oh right. I'll put the gun away. Like I trust you or something. I saw you kidnap my dad. I saw you spray him with that stuff. That was horrible. Watching that was horrible, man. Seeing your own dad roll around and puke like that.

ELIZABETH Really. So why didn't you try to help him.

STEVIE Well I'm here now, eh. I had some business to take care of, but I'm here now.

ROLLY [*opens his eyes. Sees* ELIZABETH. *Screams*] Keep away from me! Keep her away! What's this. What'd she put on me. Some kind of oil. She's gonna burn me up! Help me!

STEVIE Relax, Dad. Stay calm.

ROLLY Don't let her burn me up.

[STEVIE *moves to* ROLLY'*s side*]

STEVIE Don't worry, Dad. It was just … soup. [*to* ELIZABETH] You poured soup on him. Why? I ask you to splash him with water, and you pour a pot of soup on him. You're a pig!!

TOM Look, didn't I warn you about that kind of talk.

[TOM *takes one step towards* STEVIE]

STEVIE I'm sorry, okay?! [*he starts to cry*] Ah, man. You're just lookin' for an excuse to hurt me, aren't you.

ROLLY Hey. Stevie. It's you. [*he is free. He stands*]

STEVIE Yeah, Dad. I'm here.

[ROLLY *cuffs* STEVIE *on the head*]

ROLLY So what took you so long. Eh?! You know what I wish. I wish you were a girl. In my older years I wish I had a daughter instead of you. A daughter would have been here earlier. A daughter would take care of me in my older years. Look at her. She's a daughter. Look at all the shit she goes through for her loved ones. Why can't you be like that you little bastard.

[ROLLY *cuffs* STEVIE *repeatedly*]

STEVIE Come on, Dad. Watch it. Watch out. I've got a gun I'm trying to aim at these people. This gun is the only thing that's keeping these crazy people away, Dad. You're going to make me drop it.

ROLLY Hey that's real! Who said you could have a real gun. Since when is a real gun a thing we use. Why didn't you bring one of the toy guns we usually use.

[ROLLY *starts to cuff* STEVIE *again*]

STEVIE I mean it, Dad! Watch out. Okay. Okay. Fuck it. I'll just drop the gun. Then you'll see what happens to us here!

[DIAN *comes in*]

Hey, it's you. What are you doing here.

DIAN [*takes a gun from inside her coat*] Put that gun down, Stevie.

STEVIE I'm confused by this. Why are you here.

ELIZABETH You know her?

STEVIE Yeah. I know her.

DIAN Put the gun down. And you can go. Both of you. You can just walk away.

ROLLY She's talkin' like a cop. Is she a cop.

STEVIE She's—

DIAN Hey! Shut up! Put the gun down and leave. Or I'll use my weapon.

ELIZABETH Who is she, Stevie. Who do you think she is.

STEVIE I feel like I'm in an awkward situation here. I just came to get my dad.

DIAN And now you've got him. So leave.

ELIZABETH I want to know how you know her, Stevie.

DIAN If you make him tell you that, Elizabeth, you'll be putting us all in a very unfortunate position. Things will not turn out well. My way is better. [*to* ROLLY *and* STEVIE] Get the hell out of here!

[MIKE *swings around the basement door. Gun up*]

MIKE Everyone stay very still. [*to* STEVIE] Drop your weapon. Do it now!

ROLLY Now, he's a cop for sure. Drop it, Stevie.

[STEVIE *drops his gun.* MIKE *turns to* DIAN. *Points gun at her. She points her gun at him*]

MIKE Dian … I want you to drop your gun, too.

DIAN That's not going to happen, Mike.

JUNIOR Oh, this looks bad. This is weird. Two cops pointing guns at each other. [*he starts to sob*]

TOM What's going on here, Mike.

MIKE Can't talk now, buddy … I think my ex-partner here wants to kill me.

ELIZABETH Is that right, Dian.

DIAN It crossed my mind … Look, Mike, I think I know why you're here. But for the good of the force we better work together on this.

STEVIE Can me and my dad leave.

MIKE & DIAN Yes!

STEVIE We can go, Dad.

MIKE That's right, Dad. You can go. You can disappear back into your hole. But you have to forget everything you saw here.

DIAN And every *one* you saw here.

MIKE [*to* ROLLY] You got that?

ROLLY What about our merchandise. I'm sorry to bring it up. But it's all I've got in life. I don't have a pension, or anything.

STEVIE It's okay, Dad. You mean the videos, right? I've got them.

ROLLY Yeah? So they were right about you. You pulled a switcheroo. You brought drugs to that meeting in the alley. You sneaky little bastard. Who said you could sell drugs?! [*He cuffs* STEVIE]

STEVIE I didn't bring drugs to that meeting, Dad. I was given the drugs later.

ELIZABETH Who gave you the drugs, Stevie.

DIAN He can't answer that question. People might get hurt if he answers that question. The best thing right now is for him and his dad to leave!

MIKE [*to* ROLLY] Did you hear that.

ROLLY Yeah.

MIKE So why the fuck are you still here?!

[MIKE *is advancing on* ROLLY *and* STEVIE. ELIZABETH *puts herself in front of* ROLLY *and* STEVIE]

ELIZABETH Stay away from them. They belong to me. Stevie, I want you and your dad to stay a little longer. I'll make it worth your while.

STEVIE Is that an offer.

DIAN [*pointing her gun at* ELIZABETH] Back away, Elizabeth.

ELIZABETH You're aiming your weapon at me. What malfunctioning part of your brain is telling you to do something like that, Dian.

DIAN You're interfering in police business.

ELIZABETH You're in my mother's kitchen you demented bitch!

[MIKE *suddenly cuffs* ROLLY]

MIKE Why the fuck are you still here.

[*He cuffs* STEVIE]

How many fucking times do I have to ask you that question.

[*He cuffs them both. Fast*]

How fucking stupid are you, anyway. Are you so stupid you like pain.

TOM Hey, Mike. Not in front of my kids. Not in my house.

MIKE Can't be helped, buddy.

[*He grabs* ROLLY *with one arm.* STEVIE *with the other*]

ROLLY Okay, okay, we're leaving.

STEVIE But she made me an offer, Dad. It could be a good one. What's a little beating. A little pain. Fuck you, cop.

I'm going to tell this lady the truth about those drugs.

MIKE Sure you are.

[*He knees* STEVIE *in the groin.* STEVIE *doubles up.* MIKE *grabs* STEVIE*'s hair. Smashes his head into the refrigerator.* STEVIE *crumbles to the floor*]

ELIZABETH Ah, Jesus. I told you he belongs to me. Leave him alone!

[TOM *grabs* MIKE*'s shoulder*]

TOM Okay, that's enough, Mike.

MIKE I told you to stay out of this.

[MIKE *swings at* TOM. TOM *ducks. Grabs* MIKE*'s arm and twists it behind his back. Pushes* MIKE *face first over the kitchen table. Takes his gun away.* ELIZABETH *is moving towards* DIAN. *And what happens next happens very, very fast*]

ELIZABETH Junior.

JUNIOR What?

ELIZABETH Attack!

JUNIOR What?

ELIZABETH Attack, Junior. Kill!

JUNIOR What?! Who?!

ELIZABETH Her. Now, boy. Attack. Kill. Go for the throat.

JUNIOR Come on, Elizabeth. Give me a break here.

ELIZABETH Look, I'm telling you to kill her or suffer the consequences!

JUNIOR Okay, okay!

[JUNIOR *drops to his knees and moves towards* DIAN, *growling wildly.* DIAN *turns to face* JUNIOR]

DIAN All right, that's far enough. I'll use my weapon.

[ELIZABETH *has moved quietly and quickly behind* DIAN. *She grabs her in a bear hug, trapping* DIAN*'s arms. Lifts her off the ground*]

ELIZABETH Junior, get her gun!

[JUNIOR *grabs* DIAN*'s gun*]

DIAN Elizabeth, it's still not too late to make a deal.

ELIZABETH Sure.

[ELIZABETH *throws* DIAN *to the floor. Grabs the gun from* JUNIOR. *Puts her foot on* DIAN'*s head, pressing it to the floor. Points the gun at* DIAN'*s head*]

JUNIOR Good trick, Elizabeth. All that Junior attack and kill stuff. I was supposed to be like a mad dog, right. I didn't get it at first. Where did that come from, Elizabeth.

ELIZABETH I don't know. My subconscious, I guess. Don't worry about it.

JUNIOR Sure. But if that's how you really feel about me I'm a little—

ELIZABETH [*points gun at him*] I said don't worry about it!

JUNIOR Okay, okay …

TOM What now.

ELIZABETH Well, now we find out which one of these cops has set us up. And which one is just trying to cover up the set-up. Rolly, why aren't you picking your son off the floor.

ROLLY Fuck him.

ELIZABETH [*points gun at him*] Do it!

MIKE I'm cooled down now, Tom. You can let me up.

ELIZABETH [*points gun at him*] Keep him where he is.

DIAN You people are in over your heads. You people have crossed the line.

[ELIZABETH *stamps the floor near* DIAN'*s head.* DIAN *curls up in fear.* ROLLY *has* STEVIE *on his feet*]

ELIZABETH How you doin', Stevie.

STEVIE You know something? I don't give a fuck how I'm doing! That's how I'm doing!

ELIZABETH You were going to tell us something.

STEVIE You were gonna make me an offer. I wanna hear what it was.

ELIZABETH [*points gun at him*] Your life.

ROLLY Tricked again. I coulda told ya.

STEVIE [*to* ELIZABETH] You won't use that.

ROLLY Sure she will. She's meaner than any of them. And we're nothing to her. We're sewage. [*to* ELIZABETH] Aren't we. Shit floating in the dark. Big, fat, floating turds!

STEVIE Come on, Dad. Calm down. Have a little, you know, self-respect. I say let her shoot. Fuck her. Fuck them all. How about it.

ROLLY Yeah. Yeah, okay. Fuck you. We've been abused one too many times. We're gonna show you something here. We're gonna show you some class. Kill my kid. Go ahead. Kill him.

STEVIE [*starts to cry*] And you too, Dad. Tell her to kill you, too. Come on, Dad.

ROLLY Yeah, okay. The hell with it. Kill us both. [*starts to cry*] Come on. Whatya waiting for you big, mean, spooky woman!

[*They are approaching* ELIZABETH *arm in arm. Crying*]

STEVIE Yeah. Come on!

ROLLY Come on!

ELIZABETH [*lowers the gun*] A thousand dollars.

ROLLY What.

ELIZABETH I'll give you a thousand dollars. All Stevie has to do is tell me which one of these cops hired him to plant those drugs.

STEVIE Okay, that's more like it. That's an offer we can live with.

ROLLY Where's the money.

ELIZABETH I don't have it on me. I'll get it to you.

STEVIE Yeah. Like we trust you or somethin'.

ELIZABETH [*mocking*] Yeah. Like you got a choice or somethin'.

ROLLY Tell her. Fuck it.

STEVIE Should I.

ROLLY If I didn't think you should would I tell you you should.

[*He cuffs* STEVIE]

STEVIE Okay, okay. It was her. The lady cop.

DIAN You're making a big mistake.

[ELIZABETH *stamps the floor.* DIAN *curls up in fear*]

STEVIE But I didn't know she was a lady cop. I thought she was a lady crook. She told me she was connected to the big-time. She contacted me. Told me she wanted a favour. [*to* ROLLY] This was after we broke in here, but had to leave 'cause of the baby—

ELIZABETH Get on with it!

STEVIE Okay, she told me she wanted me to break in here again. Find our merchandise, and put the drugs there instead. If I did this I would be given things. Money. Good references. Future business dealings. Things like that. I could give you the details.

ELIZABETH That's not necessary. You can go now.

STEVIE That's it?

ROLLY We can go?

ELIZABETH Yeah.

ROLLY And you'll get that thousand dollars to us.

ELIZABETH Yes I will.

STEVIE Oh, sure you will. But you know what. I don't care. Fuck you! And everyone here! And fuck the things you're all doin'! Whatever they are! That's what I say. [*to* ROLLY] Right?

ROLLY Sure. I say that, too. But I'd still like the money.

STEVIE If we get the money, that's a good thing, I agree. But you still gotta say fuck them.

ROLLY Okay. Yeah … Fuck you! And the things you're doin'! Specially to us!

STEVIE Now all we gotta do is leave with some class.

ROLLY Come on.
    [*They leave*]

ELIZABETH Okay. Everyone up.
    [ELIZABETH *and* TOM *back away.* MIKE *and* DIAN *get up.*
    TOM *hands* MIKE*'s gun to* ELIZABETH]

TOM Here. You gotta excuse me. I'm not feeling very well.
    [*he starts off*]

ELIZABETH Are you faking illness again.

TOM No … This stuff reminds me too much of other stuff. And the other stuff reminds me of … other stuff … Bastards.

[*He leaves*]

ELIZABETH [*hands guns to* JUNIOR] Here. Take the bullets out of these for me, will you.

JUNIOR How.

ELIZABETH I don't know. Figure it out.

[JUNIOR *sits at the table*]

Why did you do this to my family, Dian. Is it because you're insane.

DIAN You were planning to do serious damage to something to which I owe a high degree of loyalty. You understand loyalty. That's one of the ways we're alike. Think of the police force as my family and you'll understand better.

ELIZABETH My family is made up of human beings. You're loyal to an institution. I'll visit you in the asylum some day and explain the difference. I assume you had the backing of at least some of your superiors.

DIAN Assume what you need to assume, Elizabeth.

JUNIOR These are unloaded. Can I go upstairs now, Elizabeth. I want to see my wife and daughter.

ELIZABETH You feeling a little sick, too?

JUNIOR Well, not sick. Just confused … and lonely.

ELIZABETH Whatever … Sure. Go on. Give them both a kiss from me.

[*He leaves.*]

DIAN [*takes out her lip balm*] Isn't that lovely. Everyone's all cozy and tucked in their beds. But who's out there protecting them while they sleep. Who stands guard and keeps the scum from the door.

ELIZABETH Who are you, Dian. What are you.

DIAN A committed social servant. Someone who believes in using all her personal resources to deal with distressing and complex issues. Look, you had to be stopped. I'm truly,

truly sorry I had to involve your mother. But a police force damaged and soiled in the public's eye is not going to be an effective player in the ongoing societal conflict! [*she begins to apply her lip balm furiously*]

ELIZABETH [*to* MIKE] Are you listening to all this.

MIKE Yeah.

ELIZABETH So what do you make of it.

DIAN What are you asking him for?! This whole thing is beyond his narrow view of life! I'm the only one with vision! The only one with imagination. I see the big picture. I see the big picture with details. I see the big picture with details that contradict what *you* see in the big picture. You think that's easy?! It's scary! It makes you do scary things sometimes!

MIKE You're nuttier than a fruitcake.

DIAN This woman here was out to destroy the force!

MIKE I don't know what force you're talking about. The one I work for just gives you a book full of laws and tells you to arrest anyone that breaks them. It's simple, really.

DIAN [*mocking*] 'It's simple, really.' God, I hate it when guys like you say that kind of shit. It's not simple. You think it's simple because you're rigid and stupid. I know it's not simple because I'm flexible and extremely intelligent.

MIKE Why do you think I followed you here. I mean, if you're so smart how come a bozo like me could figure out what you were up to. You know how? Hunches.

[DIAN *screams. Turns away.* MIKE *pursues her*]

I got that warrant to search this house, but you asked me not to use it right away. Why, I asked myself. Screw her, I said to myself. Then I got a hunch. I thought to myself, okay, I'll do what she wants for now. Then you asked me to make a deal with Elizabeth. What kind of bullshit is that, I asked myself. But because I've got this hunch I make that deal. Then you tell me you want to work alone. And at first I think this is the best thing to ever happen in my whole stinking life. Then I think, give me a fucking break! She's used me. And now she wants me out of the way. She's doing a serious number on these people. Why, I ask myself. And I tell myself, who the fuck knows or cares. This woman is a loose cannon, and she just needs to be stopped.

DIAN Walk away, Mike. Let me cut a deal with Elizabeth. She'll back off to keep her mom out of jail. The police force will be saved any more unfortunate publicity. No one gets hurt.

MIKE No!

DIAN It's the best solution.

MIKE No. No can do.

DIAN 'No!' 'No can do.' ... Why not, asshole?! Why the fuck not?! [*she is very mobile. Very agitated. Much lip balm is being applied*]

MIKE Because I've got a better plan! I got it while I was listening to you talk like a fruitcake. I came here to try and cover up your crazy scheme. But now what I want is for you to leave these people alone. Let Elizabeth make all the fuss she wants. And let the police force deal with her any way, any goddamn legal way it can.

DIAN My way is better! My way is connected to life in a complex world. It's scary. It's intuitive. Damn you! Damn you guys. Cut me some slack here. I'm the kind of cop this city needs now. I'm creative. I can arrange solutions to difficult problems in non-linear ways. I am the future! You big, dumb jerk. And I'm tough. I'm tough, too. I'm that rarest of human beings. A caring, sensitive, intelligent adult who also happens to love law and order!!

MIKE Go home, Dian. Have a bath. Take a pill. Write a letter of resignation.

DIAN I'm not quitting. I don't care what you say. I've got friends in high places. So why should I quit ... In fact, I'm asking to be made your permanent partner. We're engaged

in something here, Mike! We've got to see it through. It's big this thing we're engaged in! Big and contradictory. It's new and old. Woman and man. Daughter and father. Smart and dumb. Really, really smart! And really, really dumb!! [*She grabs his cheeks. Gives him a long hard kiss*] See you tomorrow, partner.
[*She rushes off. Out the screen door. Pause*]

MIKE [*sighs. Gestures feebly*] Ah, I'm really sorry about all—

ELIZABETH I only need to hear one thing from you now. An official confirmation that all charges against my mother, or any other member of this family pertaining to those drugs, or anything else involved in this whole obscene mess, are dropped. Can you give that to me.

MIKE Yes. I can.

ELIZABETH Thank you. I appreciate that very much. And now pay attention, Mr. Policeman, sir. I'm going to continue my campaign against police brutality. I'm going to bring your beloved police force to its knees. I'm going to start with that insane bitch. And then I'm going to destroy anyone who was even remotely involved in what she was doing to me and my family, and if that includes you, tough fucking luck!

MIKE Did you say something about police brutality? Well, you just keep right on complaining. I hate it when those awful police get brutal. I mean, who the hell are they to get brutal. All the nice people they get to deal with. All that love and affection they get from that wonderful scum out there. Why the fuck would anyone want to get brutal with that fucking, wonderful, goddamn scum. So you just make a stink about that. I'm right behind you. Goddamn right I am!
[*He leaves. Slams the door behind him.* ELIZABETH *watches him leave.* JUNIOR, *then* GAIL, *nursing the baby, then* MARY ANN, *come in behind* ELIZABETH]

ELIZABETH [*turns*] What are you doing down here.

GAIL Junior woke us up.

JUNIOR I started thinking you might need some help. I thought we should all face it together. Whatever happened.

MARY ANN What did happen.

ELIZABETH We found out who set us up.

JUNIOR It was that lady cop.

GAIL We were set up by a cop? All my worst fears are coming true. We should think about moving to the country.

MARY ANN What? Set us up? How? Why? I don't get it. Will someone explain it to me sometime. Or will it be just another one of those things I'm sort of aware of, but I don't really understand.

ELIZABETH If you want, I'll explain it to you sometime.

MARY ANN Only if you want to. Only if you think it's important that I know … someday.

ELIZABETH I do. I think it's important that just once you know something that the rest of us know. So I'll tell you.

MARY ANN But not now?

ELIZABETH That's right. Not now.

MARY ANN Good.

ELIZABETH Where's Mom.

GAIL Where's Dad.

JUNIOR Upstairs. Talking.

MARY ANN & GAIL To each other?

JUNIOR Yeah.

GAIL Dad's talking to Mom? And Mom's like … talking back to Dad? It's not like he's talking and she's pretending she doesn't hear him?

MARY ANN Or she's talking. And he's listening. But she's not really talking to him. She's talking at him. You know. In paragraphs.

GAIL Yeah. Like she was trying to reform him.

MARY ANN Like a lecture.

GAIL Yeah, a lecture.

ELIZABETH [*looks at* JUNIOR] So?

JUNIOR So. I don't know. They're talking. I think they're both talking. They're sitting on the edge of her bed.

GAIL No way.

MARY ANN Her bed? In her bedroom?

GAIL No way.

MARY ANN Talking? Both of them?

JUNIOR Yeah.

GAIL That's great. Isn't it, Mary Ann.

MARY ANN I think it is, maybe. Yeah. I think it is. It's great. I mean, it's okay. It's a good thing to talk. Right, Elizabeth?

ELIZABETH I don't know. What can come from it. What's going to happen. I've got serious reservations about that guy.

GAIL Ah. We've all got serious reservations about the guy, Elizabeth. So what. The guy's our dad. He's the dad we got. We didn't get some guy on TV. We got a kind of lunatic. But he's better than he was. I mean, when we were little … Isn't he.

ELIZABETH He tricked us. He pretended to be dying.

GAIL He didn't trick me. I knew he was faking. I knew why he was doing it, too. I thought we all knew … If you didn't know, Elizabeth, that's because you weren't around much. And when you were he had to be in his room.

MARY ANN Those sound like the same reasons why I didn't know. Know what?

GAIL That he was pretending to be sick so we wouldn't make him leave.

JUNIOR He loves you.

MARY ANN He does? Really … Loves us. He said that to someone? Who did he say that to.

JUNIOR Elizabeth.

MARY ANN Elizabeth, did Dad tell you he loves us.

ELIZABETH So what.

GAIL Sure, he loves us. Why wouldn't he love us. Why is that so hard to believe. Just because the guy's been a real asshole sometimes—

ELIZABETH You always forgive him. How do you do that. How come it's so easy for you.

GAIL I forgive you when you're an asshole. Who am I not to forgive you. Don't you forgive me.

ELIZABETH Is that the same as with Dad. That can't be the same. We've got to be talking about another word here. Forgive can't be the right word. As far as I know, Gail, you've never tried to kill me, or burn this house down, you never threw my clothes out on the street, or the hundreds of other terrorist attacks he made on this family.

MARY ANN Elizabeth, he was an alcoholic.

ELIZABETH 'Elizabeth, he was an alcoholic.' Like that's supposed to make it all right somehow. Was it the alcohol that made him leave. Made him stay away a decade. Made him come back and trick us. That's all that fucking Al. Anon. crap.

GAIL You can't do this, Elizabeth. Mom and Dad are upstairs talking to each other. That's an important event for this family. Something is happening to us right now, Elizabeth. You've got to stay in the present tense.

ELIZABETH I just don't know how … to stop. If you know a way I can stop, Gail, you better tell me.

GAIL Look, it's like everything else. Why can't you deal with Dad the way you deal with everything else in your life.

MARY ANN She means be tough.

GAIL I mean just deal with it. However you have to.

[NORA *comes in. They all look at her*]

NORA Is everything okay now, Elizabeth.

ELIZABETH Yes, Mom.

NORA I'm not going to jail.

ELIZABETH No, Mom.

NORA Good. That's good … Tom and I have been talking. I decided to talk to him. Don't make a fuss about that. I had my reasons. He told me what he'd tried to do and why. He wanted to help. I believe him. I decided to believe him. I've got my reasons, don't worry. Anyway. He wants to ask you all something. He's right out there in the hall. Come on in, Tom.

[TOM *comes in*]

Go ahead, Tom. Just ask right out loud.

[ELIZABETH *turns away*]

TOM [*quietly*] Can I stay.

[*Pause*]

NORA I don't think they heard you.

JUNIOR I heard him.

MARY ANN So did I.

GAIL She means Elizabeth.

[ELIZABETH *turns to face* TOM]

TOM [*to* ELIZABETH] Can I stay.

ELIZABETH Would that accomplish anything.

TOM We'd be together. We'd be a family.

ELIZABETH And you think that would be a good thing. You think something positive would grow out of that. I mean, what kind of family do you think we'd be with you … that we weren't without you. Stronger? Meaner? Better prepared to deal with the shit of the world? We know how you feel about that world full of shit out there. You've been telling us about it since we were kids. Obviously you haven't changed your mind. You still think we need protection. You still think that's your job.

TOM I can't help that.

ELIZABETH You still think we're weak.

TOM No. I don't.

ELIZABETH Sure you do. You make all your decisions about us based on a feeling of superiority.

TOM I don't think you're weak. I just think you've got a different kind of strength.

ELIZABETH Yeah? So what kind is it.

TOM The kind that keeps you together. It's … [*he mumbles something*]

123

NORA Love. He said love. I heard him.

GAIL So did I.

TOM The strength of love ... I need that. I want some of that, is all I'm saying. I want to be able to give over to it. And put that ugly part of me asleep forever.

ELIZABETH So how do you plan to do that.

TOM I don't really have a plan. I just want to stay. If I stay here with you I figure there's a chance for me. If I go out there alone again I won't last. The shit in my brain will meet the shit in the world and there'll be an explosion.

ELIZABETH So we're supposed to keep you here to keep you safe from the world. To keep the world safe from you.

TOM Yeah. I guess so ... But also ... so I can love you. Get loved by you. I need you all to love me so bad I can taste it. Really. I can taste the need.

ELIZABETH Where do you think love comes from.

MARY ANN Maybe that's enough for now, Elizabeth. Who can answer questions like that.

GAIL Leave her alone. She has to do this. This is what she does.

ELIZABETH [to TOM] The kind of love you're talking about. Do you think it's going to rub off on you.

TOM If I let it ... yeah.

ELIZABETH You think it's what ... hugging, kissing ... being nice?

TOM That'd be a good start.

ELIZABETH You think it's just hanging around together. Maybe going on a picnic. Maybe going skating like we used to when we were kids. We don't need you to go skating with us anymore. That would just be a luxury. At best, that would be ... a good time. We don't need you to show us a good time. We don't need you to be nice to us. If you stay we only need one thing from you ... respect.

[Long pause. They are staring at each other]

GAIL Use another word. Respect is such a sucky word, Elizabeth. It just embarrasses everyone.

ELIZABETH I don't care. It applies. Do you know what I mean, Dad. Do you have any idea what that word means. Why I used it.

TOM I do respect you. All of you. Look what you've made of yourself, Elizabeth. You're a lawyer.

ELIZABETH You're proud! We've survived. We've done better than survive. We're your women and we're chips off the old block ... Well, I don't need you to be proud of me ... You've got to do better that that. A lot better.
[*She leaves. Pause*]

MARY ANN Dad? [*she waves*] I could make you a list. I agree with most of what Elizabeth said. But I think what you really need is a list. Something you can carry around. Something that's ... real. You know, a list of things like ... no lying, no pretending, no using your 'man voice' just to get your way. Stuff like that. Do you think that would help.

TOM Maybe.

MARY ANN Okay, then. I'll make one. A list of things you can't do, and a list of things you can. Just suggestions, maybe. Nothing too strict. There's some paper upstairs, I'll bet. I'll go do it now.

TOM That's very nice of you, Mary Ann.

MARY ANN Oh no, I have to help. I have to do what I can. That's usually not much, but I still have to do it. [*to the others*] Don't I.
[*She leaves*]

GAIL Dad?

TOM Yes, honey.

GAIL I love Elizabeth and Mary Ann a lot. But it would be okay with me if you ignored them. And just tried your best ... Come on Junior, let's go to bed.

JUNIOR Great. I want to sleep for a week.

GAIL You can't. You've got to go talk to your foreman tomorrow morning.

JUNIOR You saved my job.

GAIL Unless you do something else really stupid. What have you been doing, anyway. Are you going to tell me about that. Tell me what ridiculous things you and my dad have been up to.

JUNIOR Sure. But you won't like it. You might get really mad.

GAIL Or I might just laugh.

[*They start off. Arms around each other.* GAIL *stops*]

Something else, Dad ... If you ever want to go skating with me and Gwen, that would be great. Anytime. I mean it.

[*They leave.* NORA *is sitting at the table.* TOM *joins her*]

NORA They're all different. They grew up to be different people. They never really agree about anything. That's just the way it is ... You look a little sad. And confused. Look on the bright side ... You're still here. There's still a possibility that you could stay here, and make something positive out of the experience ... Excuse me.

[*She goes out to the back porch. Shouts*]

Attention! Attention fanatics! You can stop watching now. Nobody in this house is going to prison. The problems in this house are being resolved ... I'll keep you posted!!

[*She comes back in*]

TOM I'm going to get a job.

NORA Don't do anything rash.

TOM I want to make some money. Help out.

NORA We get by. And money isn't very important around here anymore. Compared to ... other things, I mean. But if it's something you need to do ... Well, all right. But ... [*she sits across from him*] Here's some advice about that. Here's what I have to tell you about that idea. You shouldn't take a job with a lot of tension. Take a job that makes you happy. Even if it only pays a little.

[*Lights start to fade*]

We can't have you working at something that makes you tense, and angry, and resentful. We can't afford the chance

that you'll bring tension, anger, and resentment home.
Maybe you could get a job making things. Little things that
are useful. And pleasant to look at. Or a job taking care of
things. Or fixing things. Fixing things is useful and reward-
ing. Filled with satisfaction. Or a job outdoors. Outdoors is
the best environment. A job outdoors fixing and taking
care of things would be the best. Maybe you could get one
of those jobs taking care of a golf-course. That could be
very nice. Of course that's seasonal work. But maybe
seasonal work is good. You wouldn't be overdoing it that
way. You wouldn't get too tense. You'd have over half a
year to recover.
[TOM *is nodding. Lights are fading*]
What do you think. I think we should investigate the golf-
course idea. It's up to you, though. There can't be pressure.
These are only ideas. ... Suggestions. You know ... hints.
[*Blackout*]
[*End*]

Editor for the Press: Robert Wallace
Cover Design: Brenda Lavoie / Reactor
Cover Illustration: Tracy Wood
Printed in Canada

COACH HOUSE PRESS
401 (rear) Huron Street
Toronto, Canada
M5S 2G5